what's cooking

mexican

This is a Parragon Publishing book
First published in 2004

Parragon Publishing
Queen Street House
4 Queen Street
Bath BA1 1HE

ISBN: 1-40542-539-3

Printed in China

ACKNOWLEDGMENTS

PHOTOGRAPHY: Colin Bowling, Paul Forrester, and Stephen Brayne

NOTE

This book uses imperial, metric, and US measurements. Follow the same units of measurement throughout;
do not mix imperial and metric. All spoon measurements are level: teaspoons are assumed to be 5 ml
and tablespoons are assumed to be 15 ml. Unless otherwise stated, milk is assumed to be whole, eggs and
individual vegetables such as potatoes are medium, and pepper is freshly ground black pepper.

The times given for each recipe are an approximate guide only. The preparation times may differ according to
the techniques used by different people and the cooking times may vary as a result of the type of oven used.
Ovens should be preheated to the specified temperature. If using a fan-assisted oven, check the manufacturer's
instructions for adjusting the time and temperature. The preparation times include chilling
and marinating times, where appropriate.

Recipes using raw or very lightly cooked eggs should be avoided by infants, the elderly,
pregnant women, convalescents, and anyone suffering from an illness.

contents

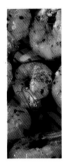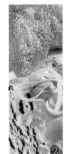

introduction

The cuisine of Mexico is a diverse and extraordinary one—a complex layering of cultures, starting with the ancient Indian civilizations and built upon by the Spanish conquest, as well as other European rulers and influences.

The soul of Mexican food lies in its ancient roots: Aztec, Toltec, Zapotec, Ohnec, and Mayan. Deeply colored, complex, rich sauces made of mild and hot chiles, seeds, herbs, and vegetables are as ancient as the cultures from which they come. Long-stewed meats, such as the Spanish contribution of pork, figure prominently in the Mexican kitchen; the broth that is produced through the cooking makes soups that fuel everyday life and add flavor and depth to dishes of beans, rice, and stews. Fish from the coastlines that cover thousands of miles and define the shape of the country are eaten cloaked in spicy pastes, scattered with chiles, and wrapped in tortillas or fragrant leaves.

Over this ancient cuisine of indigenous foods and techniques lies a veneer of Spanish propriety and European tradition, as well as the imports from Spain: wheat (for those flour tortillas and the crusty bread rolls, *bolillos*), domesticated animals whose milk added cheese to the menu, and the pig! With the abundant fat provided by the pig, frying became possible, adding a new dimension to the cooking methods.

TORTILLAS

The *tortilla*—a thin crêpe-like flat bread—is eaten at nearly every meal throughout Mexico. Served in the same way as bread to accompany dishes, they are also wrapped around food as an eating utensil.

In the north, wheat or flour tortillas will be the ones you will find most often; in the south they will be corn, sometimes blue corn. Tortilla may be tiny or huge, eaten fresh off the griddle (*comal*) or filled and fried; they form the basis of the foods of Mexico.

Wrapped around any filling, a corn tortilla becomes a taco; a flour tortilla a *burrito*. Fresh and warm, a corn tortilla is a soft *taco*; fried to a crisp it is a crisp taco. A flat crisply fried tortilla is a *tostada*—top them with a layer of warm refried beans, cheese, pickled chiles or salsa, salad, and morsels of meat or vegetables.

Stale corn tortillas are never thrown away in the frugal Mexican kitchen, and the cuisine is all the better for it. Dipped into spicy sauces, then rolled around various fillings, they make the wonderful casserole that is called *enchiladas*, or fried and layered with sauce they are called *chilaquiles*.

Most of us are familiar with tortilla chips—which are widely available in packages but are at their best when freshly made from stale corn tortillas.

BEANS

Beans, too, are staple, along with rice and chiles. In every marketplace café (*fonda*) and home kitchen, you'll find pots and *cazuelas* of simmering beans, ready to be eaten in all their guises, or just from a bowl with a few tortillas to wrap around them to satisfy hunger.

Throughout Mexico, the types of beans vary delightfully, from the tender pale pink beans of the north, such as pinto, to the inky black beans of the south. Beans that are puréed and cooked in fat and spices are called refried beans, though they are not really fried at all but cooked down to an intense paste in a puddle of shortening or, as is used more commonly these days, vegetable oil.

CHILES

Next to tortillas and beans, it is chiles that define Mexican food. They offer flavors, textures, colors, and aromas, as well as heat, and keep the often monotonous diet lively. They are consumed raw and cooked, sliced and stewed, stuffed and puréed, soaked and fried, and are eaten at every meal, usually in the form of a salsa to add as desired. They are rich in antioxidant vitamins and will clear your sinuses pronto, not to mention their alleged aphrodisiac qualities.

Understandably, chiles can intimidate—they can be searingly hot, and should be added a little at a time. Mild chiles are generally eaten red and dried, though Mexicans also dote on crushed hot red chiles—usually a dried cayenne. Mild chiles, such as *pasilla*, *ancho*, *mulato*, and *negro*, make up the distinctive flavorful mixture sold simply on our spice shelf as "mild chili powder".

Most fresh chiles are hot and hotter. *Jalapeño* are probably most often eaten—a good all-purpose little chile with a nice fiery heat and delicious flavor. *Serrano* is another popular fresh chile. In the Caribbean region, *habanero* and Scotch bonnet chile peppers add their distinctive fire.

Two milder chiles, the Anaheim and *poblano*, are utterly delicious eaten stuffed, as you would a bell pepper; if unavailable, use ordinary green bell peppers, roasted and marinated with a chopped fresh hot chile or two to enliven them.

Bottled hot seasonings are ubiquitous, too; you'll find one on practically every table as well as kitchen shelf—a nice jolt of tangy fire for those who dare.

OTHER FLAVORINGS

Mexican spicing, however, is not only limited to chiles: cinnamon, cloves, black pepper, unsweetened cocoa, and especially cumin are used with enthusiasm, as are the herbs of oregano, marjoram, mint, *epazote* (a wild herb sold in Latin markets), and fresh cilantro. Roasted onion and whole garlic cloves are often crushed to form the basis of a sauce, and wedges of lime or lemon are served with soups, meats, fish, almost everything, Mediterranean-style.

MEXICAN STYLE

Meals in Mexico are a never-ending fiesta. The main meal, the *comida corrida*, is served, Spanish-style, in the afternoon. Breakfast may either be a light one of hot chocolate or coffee with sweet rolls or *churros* to dip in, or a hearty late breakfast *almuerzo*, often consisting of the exquisite egg dishes for which Mexico is well known. The markets and their *fondas*, *cantinas*, and *taquerias* beckon you with their irresistible aromas, convincing you that you are indeed hungry, and an endless parade of tacos, tostadas, enchiladas, burritos, soups, shellfish, and broiled fish tantalize the palate.

And if your appetite is jaded from the sultry heat and feasting, and you don't have room for even one more burrito, persuade yourself to nibble a reviving snack—fresh fruits sprinkled with hot red pepper and served with a squeeze of lime juice. After that you'll be ready for anything!

soups & appetizers

Start your meal in authentic Mexican style with a bowl of homemade soup. Mexican soups are distinctive and varied, ranging from light soups of plain stock served with a spoonful of salsa and a little lime, to hearty one-bowl meals such as Pozole (see page 26). Whatever your soup, expect to find it served with a wedge of lime, lemon, or orange, a sprinkling of pungent fresh cilantro, and a hint of hot chile.

Little nibbles, too, are an important part of any Mexican meal. The world-famous Guacamole (see page 29)—mashed avocado with seasonings and spices—makes a perfect appetizer, delicious with crunchy tortilla chips and a cooling Mexican beer or a shot of tequila. Spicy-Sweet Meat Empanadas (see page 57), filled with savory meat, aromatic spices, and nuts, are as moreish as they are unusual, and you can keep them in your freezer ready to take out for an impromptu party, at any time.

With its thousands of miles of coastline, seafood cocktails and marinated fish make cooling, refreshing, and light appetizers to start a Mexican feast. Alternatively, you could serve tiny tacos, rolls of tortillas filled with mouth-watering Mexican mixtures, or a salad of raw vegetables spiced with chiles. Whatever your taste, you'll be enticed by the recipes in this chapter.

yucatan citrus soup

serves 4

10 minutes

45 minutes

2 onions, unpeeled
15 large garlic cloves, unpeeled
1 tbsp virgin olive oil
generous 1 quart vegetable, chicken,
   or fish stock
1 cup water
8 ripe tomatoes, diced
pinch of dried oregano
1 fresh green chile, such as jalapeño
   or serrano, seeded and chopped
pinch of ground cumin
$\frac{1}{2}$ tsp finely grated grapefruit rind

$\frac{1}{2}$ tsp finely grated lime rind
$\frac{1}{2}$ tsp finely grated orange rind
salt and pepper
juice and diced flesh of 2 limes
juice of 1 orange
juice of 1 grapefruit

to garnish

tortilla strips, fried until crisp, or
   tortilla chips
2 tbsp chopped fresh cilantro

Roasted onion and garlic are combined with tangy citrus flavors to create a soup full of tantalizing tastes.

Halve one unpeeled onion. Peel and finely chop the other.

Heat an unoiled large, heavy-bottomed skillet. Add the unpeeled onion halves and garlic and cook over medium–high heat until the skins char and the onions are caramelized on their cut sides; the garlic should be soft on the inside. Remove from the skillet and let cool slightly.

Meanwhile, heat the oil in a pan. Add the remaining onion and lightly cook for 5 minutes, or until softened. Add the stock and water and bring to a boil. Reduce the heat and simmer for a few minutes.

Peel the charred onion and garlic, then coarsely chop. Add to the simmering soup, together with the tomatoes, oregano, chile, and cumin. Cook for 15 minutes, stirring the soup occasionally.

Add the citrus rind and season to taste with salt and pepper. Simmer for an additional 2 minutes. Remove the pan from the heat and stir in the lime flesh and citrus juices.

Ladle into soup bowls, garnish with fried tortilla strips and chopped cilantro, and serve.

spicy gazpacho

serves 4–6

15 minutes,
plus 3 hours chilling

1 cucumber
2 green bell peppers
6 ripe flavorful tomatoes
1/2 fresh hot chile
1/2–1 onion, finely chopped
3–4 garlic cloves, chopped
4 tbsp extra-virgin olive oil
1/4–1/2 tsp ground cumin
2–4 tsp sherry vinegar, or a
    combination of balsamic vinegar
    and wine vinegar

4 tbsp chopped fresh cilantro
2 tbsp chopped fresh parsley
1 1/4 cups vegetable or
    chicken stock
2 1/2 cups tomato juice or canned
    crushed tomatoes
salt and pepper

to serve

ice cubes
crusty bread

*This classic Spanish cold
soup is given a Mexican twist
by adding chiles and fresh
cilantro. Serve with chunks of
bread for a refreshing
start to a meal.*

Cut the cucumber in half lengthwise, then cut into quarters. Remove the seeds with a teaspoon, then dice the flesh. Cut the bell peppers in half, remove the cores and seeds, then dice the flesh.

If you prefer to peel the tomatoes, place in a heatproof bowl, pour boiling water over to cover, and let stand for 30 seconds. Drain and plunge into cold water. The skins will then slide off easily. Cut the tomatoes in half, seed if wished, then chop the flesh. Seed and chop the chile.

In a bowl, combine half the cucumber, green bell pepper, tomatoes, and onion, then place in a food processor or blender with the chile, garlic, oil, cumin, vinegar, and herbs. Process with enough stock to form a smooth purée.

Pour the puréed soup into a bowl and stir in the remaining stock and tomato juice. Add the remaining cucumber, green bell pepper, tomatoes, and onion, stirring well. Season to taste with salt and pepper, then cover and chill for a few hours.

variation

*Freeze tomato juice ice cubes
as a delicious alternative.*

Put some ice cubes into each bowl before ladling in the gazpacho and serve with bread.

spicy zucchini soup with rice & lime

serves 4

5 minutes

15 minutes

2 tbsp vegetable oil
4 garlic cloves, thinly sliced
1–2 tbsp mild red chili powder
1/4–1/2 tsp ground cumin
1 1/4 quarts chicken, vegetable, or beef stock

2 zucchini, cut into bite-size chunks
4 tbsp long-grain rice
salt and pepper
fresh oregano sprigs, to garnish
lime wedges, to serve (optional)

Mild red chili powder and pan-browned garlic give flavor to this simple, homely soup. Quick to make, it's ideal for a light lunch.

Heat the oil in a heavy-bottomed pan. Add the garlic and cook for 2 minutes, or until softened and just beginning to change color. Add the chili powder and cumin and cook over medium–low heat for 1 minute.

Stir in the stock, zucchini, and rice, then cook over medium–high heat for 10 minutes, or until the zucchini are just tender and the rice is cooked through. Season the soup to taste with salt and pepper.

Ladle into soup bowls, garnish with oregano sprigs, and serve with lime wedges, if wished.

cook's tip

Choose zucchini that are firm to the touch and have shiny skin. They should not be too large.

variation

Instead of rice, use rice-shaped pasta, such as orzo or semone de melone, or very thin pasta known as fideo. Use yellow summer squash instead of the zucchini and add cooked pinto beans in place of the rice. Diced tomatoes also make a tasty addition.

mexican vegetable soup with tortilla chips

serves 4–6

10 minutes

40 minutes

2 tbsp vegetable or virgin olive oil

1 onion, finely chopped

4 garlic cloves, finely chopped

1/4–1/2 tsp ground cumin

2–3 tsp mild chili powder, such as ancho or New Mexico

1 carrot, sliced

1 waxy potato, diced

12 oz/350 g diced fresh or canned tomatoes

1 zucchini, diced

1/4 small cabbage, shredded

4 cups vegetable or chicken stock or water

1 corn cob, the kernels cut off the cob, or canned corn kernels

about 10 green or string beans, cut into bite-size lengths

salt and pepper

to serve

4–6 tbsp chopped fresh cilantro

salsa of your choice or chopped fresh chile, to taste

tortilla chips

Crisp tortilla chips act as croutons in this hearty vegetable soup, which is found throughout Mexico. Add cheese to melt in, if you wish, and make the soup as hot tasting as you like!

Heat the oil in a heavy-bottomed skillet or pan. Add the onion and garlic and cook for a few minutes until softened, then sprinkle in the cumin and chili powder. Stir in the carrot, potato, tomatoes, zucchini, and cabbage and cook for 2 minutes, stirring the mixture occasionally.

Pour in the stock. Cover and cook over medium heat for 20 minutes, or until the vegetables are tender.

Add extra water if necessary, then stir in the corn and beans and cook for an additional 5–10 minutes, or until the beans are tender. Season the soup to taste with salt and pepper, bearing in mind that the tortilla chips may be salty.

Ladle the soup into soup bowls and sprinkle each portion with chopped cilantro. Top with a little salsa, then add a handful of tortilla chips.

crab & cabbage soup

serves 4

25 minutes

35 minutes

¼ cabbage

1 lb/450 g ripe tomatoes

4 cups fish stock or water mixed with 1–2 fish bouillon cubes

1 onion, thinly sliced

1 small carrot, diced

4 garlic cloves, finely chopped

6 tbsp chopped fresh cilantro

1 tsp mild chili powder, such as New Mexico

1 whole cooked crab or 6–8 oz/175–225 g cooked crabmeat

1 tbsp torn fresh oregano leaves

salt and pepper

to serve

1–2 limes, cut into wedges

salsa of your choice

From the Veracruz region, this delicious soup uses fresh crabmeat to add a rich flavor to a mildly spicy vegetable and fish broth.

Cut out any thick stalk from the cabbage, then finely shred using a large knife. To peel the tomatoes, place in a heatproof bowl, pour boiling water over to cover, and let stand for 30 seconds. Drain and plunge into cold water. The skins will then slide off easily. Chop the tomatoes.

Place the tomatoes and stock in a pan with the cabbage, onion, carrot, garlic, cilantro, and chili powder. Bring to a boil, then reduce the heat and simmer for 20 minutes, or until the vegetables are just tender.

Remove the crabmeat from the whole crab, if using. Twist off the legs and claws and crack with a heavy knife. Remove the flesh from the legs with a skewer; leave the cracked claws intact, if wished. Remove the body section from the main crab shell and remove the meat, discarding the stomach bag and feathery gills.

Add the oregano and crabmeat to the pan and let simmer for 10–15 minutes to combine the flavors. Season the mixture to taste with salt and pepper.

Ladle into deep soup bowls and serve with lime wedges. Hand round the salsa separately.

mexican fish & roasted tomato soup

serves 4

20 minutes

30–60 minutes

5 ripe tomatoes

5 garlic cloves, unpeeled

1 lb 2 oz/500 g red snapper, cut into chunks

4 cups fish stock or water mixed with 1–2 fish bouillon cubes

2–3 tbsp olive oil

1 onion, chopped

2 fresh green chiles, such as serrano, seeded and thinly sliced

lime wedges, to serve

Mexico's long shoreline yields an abundance of fish and shellfish, which are often turned into spicy, satisfying soups.

Heat an unoiled heavy-bottomed skillet. Add the tomatoes and garlic and char over high heat or under a preheated hot broiler. The skins of the vegetables should blacken and the flesh inside should be tender. Alternatively, place the tomatoes and garlic in a roasting pan and bake in a preheated oven at 375°F/190°C for 40 minutes.

Let the tomatoes and garlic cool, then remove the skins and coarsely chop, combining them with any juices from the skillet or roasting pan. Set aside.

Poach the fish in the stock in a deep skillet or pan over medium heat until it is just opaque and slightly firm. Remove from the heat and set aside.

Heat the oil in a separate deep skillet or pan. Add the onion and cook for 5 minutes, or until softened. Strain in the cooking liquid from the fish, then stir in the tomatoes and garlic.

Bring to a boil, then reduce the heat and simmer for 5 minutes to combine the flavors. Add the chiles.

Divide chunks of the poached fish between soup bowls, ladle over the hot soup, and serve with lime wedges for squeezing over the top.

chicken, avocado & chipotle soup

serves 4

10 minutes

5 minutes

1¼ quarts chicken stock

2–3 garlic cloves, finely chopped

1–2 dried chipotle chiles, cut into very thin strips (see Cook's Tip)

1 avocado

lime or lemon juice, for tossing

3–5 scallions, thinly sliced

12–14 oz/350–400 g cooked chicken breast meat, torn or cut into shreds or thin strips

2 tbsp chopped fresh cilantro

to serve

1 lime, cut into wedges

handful of tortilla chips (optional)

This soup evolved from the foodstalls that line the streets of Tlalpan, a suburb of Mexico City: rich avocado, shreds of chicken, and the smoky hit of chipotle make it special.

Place the stock in a large, heavy-bottomed pan with the garlic and chiles and bring to a boil.

Meanwhile, cut the avocado in half around the pit. Twist apart, then remove the pit with a knife. Carefully peel off the skin, dice the flesh, and toss in lime juice to prevent discoloration.

Arrange the scallions, chicken, avocado, and cilantro in the bottom of 4 soup bowls or in a large serving bowl.

Ladle hot stock over and serve with lime wedges and a handful of tortilla chips, if wished.

cook's tip

Chipotle chiles are smoked and dried jalapeño chiles. They are available canned or dried and add a distinctive smoky flavor to dishes as well as a powerful heat. Use chipotles canned in adobo marinade for this recipe, if possible. Drain the canned version before using. Dried chipotles need to be reconstituted before using (see page 100).

variation

Add 14 oz/400 g canned, drained chickpeas to the bowls with the scallions, chicken, avocado, and cilantro.

big pot of simmered meat

serves 6

25 minutes,
plus 30 minutes cooling

3 hours

4 lb 8 oz/2 kg beef, pork, and/or chicken for stewing—any combination or just one type

2 onions, chopped

1 whole garlic bulb, divided into cloves and peeled

several sprigs of fresh herbs, such as parsley, oregano, and cilantro

1 carrot, sliced

1–2 bouillon cubes

salt and pepper

freshly cooked macaroni or thin noodles

finely sliced scallions, to garnish

The Mexican kitchen traditionally simmers big chunks of meat, which gives two meals in one: tender boiled meat for tacos or enchiladas, as well as a hearty rich stock for soups and rice.

variation

For a simple soup to make from the strained stock, cook diced zucchini in the stock with a cinnamon stick. Remove and discard the cinnamon stick, then serve the soup with a wedge of lime, a dash of salsa to taste, and a sprinkling of fresh cilantro.

Place the meat in a large pan and cover with cold water. Bring to a boil, then skim off the scum that rises to the surface. Reduce the heat and add the onions, garlic, herbs, and carrot. Simmer, covered, for 1 hour. (If using a combination of meat and chicken, cook the meat first for 1 hour, then add the chicken.)

Add the bouillon cubes and salt and pepper to taste. Continue to simmer over very low heat for 2 hours, or until the meat is very tender.

Remove from the heat and let the meat cool in the stock. Remove the meat using a slotted spoon. Transfer to a board, remove the skin from the chicken, and shred; set aside. Skim the fat from the stock, or let chill, then remove the fat by simply lifting it off. Strain the soup for a clearer soup. Reheat before serving.

When ready to serve, spoon the hot macaroni or noodles into soup bowls, then top with the shredded meat and ladle over the soup. Garnish with sliced scallions and serve.

beef & vegetable soup

serves 4–6

15 minutes

20 minutes

8 oz/225 g tomatoes

2 corn cobs

1 carrot, thinly sliced

1 onion, chopped

1–2 small waxy potatoes, diced

1/4 cabbage, thinly sliced

4 cups beef stock or soup, following the recipe on page 22, or use a chilled ready-made stock

1/4 tsp ground cumin

1/4 tsp mild chili powder

1/4 tsp paprika

8 oz/225 g cooked beef (preferably from the recipe on page 22), cut into bite-size pieces

3–4 tbsp chopped fresh cilantro (optional)

hot salsa, such as Scorched Chile Salsa (see page 103), to serve

A wonderful meal-in-a-bowl, this soup is ideal for a winter supper or lunch. The beefy flavor, enhanced with spices, is very warming.

cook's tip

To thicken the soup and give it a flavor of the popular Mexican steamed dumpling known as a tamale (see page 139), add a few tablespoons of masa harina (whole ground white or yellow corn), mixed into a thinnish paste with a little water, with the corn, spices, and beef. Stir well, then cook until thickened.

To peel the tomatoes, place in a heatproof bowl, pour boiling water over to cover, and let stand for 30 seconds. Drain and plunge into cold water. The skins will then slide off easily. Chop the tomatoes.

Using a large knife, cut the corn cobs into 1-inch/2.5-cm pieces.

Place the tomatoes, carrot, onion, potatoes, cabbage, and stock in a large, heavy-bottomed pan. Bring to a boil, then reduce the heat and simmer for 10–15 minutes, or until the vegetables are tender.

Add the corn pieces, the cumin, chili powder, paprika, and beef pieces. Return to a boil over medium heat.

Ladle into soup bowls and serve sprinkled with cilantro, if using, with salsa handed round separately.

pozole

serves 4

45 minutes

2 hours

1 lb/450 g pork for stewing, such as lean belly

½ small chicken

about 1¾ quarts water

1 chicken bouillon cube

1 whole garlic bulb, divided into cloves but not peeled

1 onion, chopped

2 bay leaves

1 lb/450 g canned or cooked hominy or chickpeas

¼–½ tsp ground cumin

salt and pepper

to serve

½ small cabbage, thinly shredded

fried pork skin

dried oregano leaves

dried chili flakes

lime wedges

tortilla chips (optional)

The dish of hulled maize kernels—hominy—simmered in rich stock is eaten all over Mexico, and is served with lots of fresh garnishes: shredded cabbage, onion, fried tortilla, or crisp-fried pork skin (chicharrones), and, of course, chiles and lime wedges.

Place the pork and chicken in a large pan. Add enough water to fill the pan. (Do not worry about having too much stock—it can be used in other dishes, and freezes well.)

Bring to a boil, then skim off the scum that rises to the surface. Reduce the heat and add the bouillon cube, garlic, onion, and bay leaves. Simmer, covered, over medium–low heat for 1½–2 hours, or until the pork and chicken are both tender and cooked through.

Using a slotted spoon, remove the pork and chicken from the soup and let cool. When cool enough to handle, remove the chicken flesh from the bones and cut into small pieces. Cut the pork into bite-size pieces. Set aside.

Skim the fat off the soup and discard the bay leaves. Add the hominy or chickpeas, cumin, and salt and pepper to taste. Bring to a boil.

To serve, place a little pork and chicken in soup bowls. Top with cabbage, fried pork skin, oregano, and chili flakes, then spoon in the hot soup. Serve with lime wedges and tortilla chips, if wished.

authentic guacamole

serves 4

15 minutes

1 ripe tomato

2 limes

2–3 ripe small to medium avocados or 1–2 large ones

1/4–1/2 onion, finely chopped

pinch of ground cumin

pinch of mild chili powder

1/2–1 fresh green chile, such as jalapeño or serrano, seeded and finely chopped

1 tbsp finely chopped fresh cilantro leaves, plus extra to garnish (optional)

salt (optional)

tortilla chips, to serve (optional)

Guacamole is at its best when freshly made, with enough texture to really taste the avocado. Serve as a sauce for anything Mexican, or dip into it with vegetable sticks or tortilla chips.

cook's tip

Avocados grow in abundance in Mexico, and Guacamole is used to add richness and flavor to all manner of dishes. Try spooning it into soups, especially chicken or seafood, spreading it into sandwiches, or stirring it into pan drippings for a rich avocado sauce.

To peel the tomato, place in a heatproof bowl, pour boiling water over to cover, and let stand for 30 seconds. Drain and plunge into cold water. The skin will then slide off easily. Cut in half, seed, and chop the flesh.

Squeeze the juice from the limes into a small nonmetallic bowl. Cut one avocado in half around the pit. Twist apart, then remove the pit with a knife. Carefully peel off the skin, dice the flesh, and toss in the bowl of lime juice to prevent discoloration. Repeat with the remaining avocados. Coarsely mash the avocados.

Add the tomato, onion, cumin, chili powder, chile, and cilantro to the avocados. If using as a dip for tortilla chips, do not add salt. If using as a sauce, add salt to taste.

To serve the guacamole as a dip, transfer to a serving dish, garnish with finely chopped cilantro, and serve with tortilla chips.

roasted cheese with salsa

serves 4

10 minutes

15 minutes

8 oz/225 g mozzarella, fresh romano, or Mexican queso oaxaca cheese

1 cup Salsa Cruda (see page 97) or other good salsa

1/2–1 onion, finely chopped

8 soft corn tortillas, to serve

The combination of melting cheese and hot salsa is completely irresistible! Called oueso fundito *in Mexico, it is often prepared on the grill to nibble on while you wait for the rest of the meal to cook.*

Preheat the oven to 400°F/200°C or preheat the broiler to medium. To warm the tortillas ready for serving, heat an unoiled nonstick skillet, add a tortilla, and heat through, sprinkling with a few drops of water as it heats. Wrap in foil or a clean dish towel to keep warm. Repeat with the other tortillas.

Cut the cheese into chunks or slabs and arrange them in a shallow oven-proof dish or in individual dishes.

Spoon the salsa over the cheese to cover and place in the preheated oven or under the hot broiler. Cook until the cheese melts and is bubbling, lightly browning in places.

Sprinkle with chopped onion to taste and serve with the warmed tortillas for dipping. Serve immediately as the melted cheese turns stringy when cold and becomes difficult to eat.

cook's tip

Queso oaxaca, *Oaxaca's famous string cheese, is the authentic cheese to use, but mozzarella or romano make excellent substitutes, since they produce the right effect when melted.*

variation

Use Salsa Verde (see page 103) in place of the red tomato salsa, and serve with tortilla chips for dipping into the roasted cheese rather than soft corn tortillas.

seafood cocktail
à la veracruz

serves 6

50 minutes

15 minutes

4 cups fish stock or water mixed
   with 1 fish bouillon cube

2 bay leaves

1 onion, chopped

3–5 garlic cloves, cut into big chunks

1 lb 8 oz/675 g mixed raw seafood,
   such as shrimp in their shells,
   scallops, squid rings, pieces of
   squid tentacles, etc.

¾ cup tomato ketchup

4 tbsp Mexican hot sauce

generous pinch of ground cumin

6–8 tbsp chopped fresh cilantro

4 tbsp lime juice, plus extra
   for tossing

salt

1 avocado, to garnish

*"Mariscos!" cry the signs in brightly
painted colors along Mexico's
beaches and sea fronts, wherever
fresh seafood is served. This is a
typical salad dish you'll find on
offer, full of spicy flavors.*

Place the stock in a large, heavy-bottomed pan and add the bay leaves, half
the onion, and all the garlic. Bring to a boil, then reduce the heat and
simmer for 10 minutes, or until the onion and garlic are soft and the stock
tastes flavorful.

Add the seafood in the order of the amount of cooking time required.
Most small pieces of shellfish take a very short time to cook, and can be
added together. Cook for 1 minute, then remove the pan from the heat.
Allow the seafood to finish cooking by standing in the cooling stock.

When the stock has cooled, remove the seafood from the stock with a
slotted spoon. Shell the shrimp and any other shellfish. Set the stock aside
until required.

Combine the ketchup, hot sauce, and cumin in a bowl. Reserve a quarter
of the sauce mixture for serving. Add the seafood to the bowl with the
remaining onion, cilantro, lime juice, and about 1 cup of the reserved fish
stock. Stir carefully to mix and season to taste with salt.

Peel and pit the avocado, then dice the flesh. Toss gently in lime juice to
prevent discoloration. Serve the cocktail in individual bowls, garnished with
the avocado, and topped with a spoonful of the reserved sauce.

citrus-marinated fish

serves 4

30 minutes, plus 5 hours chilling

1 lb/450 g white-fleshed fish fillets, cut into bite-size chunks

juice of 6–8 limes

2–3 ripe flavorful tomatoes, diced

3 fresh green chiles, such as jalapeño or serrano, seeded and thinly sliced

½ tsp dried oregano

⅓ cup extra-virgin olive oil

1 small onion, finely chopped

salt and pepper

2 tbsp chopped fresh cilantro

Ceviche, as it is called in Mexico, is one of the country's classic dishes: raw fish, cured in a bath of citrus juices, chiles, and aromatics. It is sublime made with the freshest fish possible.

Place the fish in a nonmetallic dish, add the lime juice, and mix well. Cover and let chill in the refrigerator for 5 hours, or until the fish looks opaque. (Do not leave too long, otherwise the texture will spoil.) Turn from time to time so that the lime juice permeates the fish.

An hour before serving, add the tomatoes, chiles, oregano, oil, and onion. Season to taste with salt and pepper. Return to the refrigerator.

About 15 minutes before serving, remove from the refrigerator so that the oil comes to room temperature. Serve sprinkled with cilantro.

cook's tip

This dish makes an elegant appetizer, served layered with rounds of crisp tortillas, like a stacked tostada. It also makes a refreshing lunch, served piled up in halved avocados, surrounded by sliced mango, papaya, or grapefruit.

variation

Serve garnished with cooked marinated artichoke hearts, or drained artichokes from a can or jar.

salpicon of crab

serves 4

15 minutes

—

¹/₄ red onion, chopped
¹/₂–1 fresh green chile, seeded
   and chopped
juice of ¹/₂ lime
1 tbsp cider or other fruit vinegar,
   such as raspberry
1 tbsp chopped fresh cilantro
1 tbsp extra-virgin olive oil

8–12 oz/225–350 g fresh crabmeat
lettuce leaves, to serve

to garnish

1 avocado
lime juice, for tossing
1–2 ripe tomatoes
3–5 radishes

This lightly spiced crab salad is a cooling treat for a hot day. Eat it with crisp tortilla chips, or wrapped in a tender warm corn tortilla.

variation

For a toasted crab salad sandwich, split open a long roll or baguette and heap on crab salad. Top with a generous layer of cheese. Place the open roll under the broiler to melt the cheese. Spread the toasted plain side with mayonnaise and close up. Cut and serve with salsa.

In a large, nonmetallic bowl, combine the red onion with the chile, lime juice, vinegar, cilantro, and oil. Add the crabmeat and toss the ingredients lightly together.

To make the garnish, cut the avocado in half around the pit. Twist apart, then remove the pit with a knife. Carefully peel off the skin and slice the flesh. Toss the avocado gently in lime juice to prevent discoloration.

Halve the tomatoes, then remove the cores and seeds. Dice the flesh. Thinly slice the radishes.

Arrange the crab salad on a bed of lettuce leaves and garnish with the avocado, tomatoes, and radishes. Serve at once.

pickled cauliflower, carrots & chiles

serves 6

30 minutes

8–12 minutes

3 tbsp vegetable oil

1 onion, thinly sliced

5 garlic cloves, cut into slivers

3 carrots, thinly sliced

2 fresh green chiles, such as jalapeño or serrano, seeded and cut into strips

1 small cauliflower, broken into florets or cut into bite-size chunks

½ red bell pepper, seeded and diced or cut into strips

1 celery stalk, cut into bite-size pieces

½ tsp dried oregano

1 bay leaf

¼ tsp ground cumin

⅓ cup cider vinegar

salt and pepper

In Mexican cantinas, these pickled vegetables are munched alongside a stack of warm buttered tortillas and washed down with glasses of chilled lager, or maybe a little shot of tequila and a wedge of lime.

Heat the oil in a heavy-bottomed skillet. Add the onion, garlic, carrots, chiles, cauliflower, red bell pepper, and celery and lightly cook for 3 minutes, or until beginning to soften.

Add the oregano, bay leaf, cumin, cider vinegar, and salt and pepper to taste. Add enough water to just cover the vegetables. Cook for an additional 5–10 minutes, or just long enough for the vegetables to be tender but still firm to the bite.

Adjust the seasoning, adding more vinegar if needed. Let cool and serve as a relish. The mixture will keep for up to 2 weeks, if covered and stored in the refrigerator.

cheese & bean quesadillas

serves 4–6

10 minutes

10 minutes

8 flour tortillas
vegetable oil, for oiling
½ quantity Mexican Refried Beans
    (see page 147) or Refried Beans
    (see page 145), warmed with a
    little water
7 oz/200 g Cheddar cheese, grated

1 onion, chopped
½ bunch fresh cilantro leaves,
    chopped, plus extra leaves to
    garnish (optional)
1 quantity Salsa Cruda (see page 97)

These bite-size rolls are made from flour tortillas filled with a scrumptious mixture of refried beans, melted cheese, fresh cilantro, and salsa.

First make the tortillas pliable, by warming them gently in a lightly oiled nonstick skillet.

Remove the tortillas from the skillet and quickly spread with a layer of warmed beans. Top each tortilla with grated cheese, onion, cilantro, and a spoonful of salsa. Roll up tightly.

Just before serving, heat the nonstick skillet over medium heat, sprinkling lightly with a drop or two of water. Add the tortilla rolls, cover the skillet, and heat through until the cheese melts. Allow to lightly brown, if wished.

Remove from the skillet and slice each roll, on the diagonal, into about 4 bite-size pieces. Serve the dish at once, garnished with cilantro, if wished.

cook's tip

Flour tortillas can also be warmed in the microwave, but take care not to heat them for too long as they can become leathery.

variation

Top each tortilla with florets of lightly cooked broccoli or sautéed sliced exotic mushrooms instead of the beans, for a more lightweight filling if you wish.

Cooked drained black beans can also be substituted for the refried beans— use with Chipotle Salsa (see page 99) instead of the Salsa Cruda for a subtle change of flavor.

chorizo & artichoke
heart quesadillas

serves 4–6

15 minutes,
plus 20 minutes standing

25 minutes

1 chorizo sausage

1 large mild fresh green chile or
green bell pepper (optional)

8–10 marinated artichoke hearts or
canned artichoke hearts, drained
and diced

4 soft corn tortillas, warmed

2 garlic cloves, finely chopped

12 oz/350 g cheese, grated

1 tomato, diced

2 scallions, thinly sliced

1 tbsp chopped fresh cilantro

*Ideal to serve with drinks, these
bites are incredibly easy to make—
simply top flat tortillas with the
ingredients of your choice, pop them
under the broiler, then
serve in wedges.*

Preheat the broiler to medium. Dice the chorizo. Heat a heavy-bottomed skillet, add the chorizo, and cook until it browns in places.

If using the chile or green bell pepper, place under the hot broiler and cook for 10 minutes, or until the skin is charred and the flesh softened. Place in a plastic bag, twist to seal well, and let stand for 20 minutes. Carefully remove the skins from the chile or bell pepper with a knife, then seed and chop the flesh.

Arrange the browned chorizo and artichoke hearts on the corn tortillas, then transfer half to a cookie sheet.

Sprinkle with the chopped garlic, then the grated cheese. Place under the hot broiler and cook until the cheese melts and sizzles. Repeat with the remaining tortillas.

Sprinkle the warmed tortillas with the tomato, scallions, chile or bell pepper, if using, and the cilantro. Cut into wedges. Serve immediately.

shrimp on
crisp tortilla wedges

serves 8–10

30 minutes,
plus 4 hours chilling

15 minutes

1 lb 2 oz/500 g cooked, shelled
  shrimp
4 garlic cloves, finely chopped
1/2 tsp mild chili powder
1/2 tsp ground cumin
juice of 1 lime
1 ripe tomato, diced

salt
6 soft corn tortillas
vegetable oil, for frying
2 avocados
generous 3/4 cup sour cream
mild chili powder, to garnish
lime wedges, to serve

A winning combination of textures and flavors, spiced shrimp and creamy avocado are served on crisply fried tortilla wedges to make an irresistible appetizer.

Place the shrimp in a nonmetallic bowl with the garlic, chili powder, cumin, lime juice, and tomato. Add salt to taste and stir gently to mix. Cover and let chill in the refrigerator for at least 4 hours or overnight to allow the flavors to mingle.

Cut the tortillas into wedges. Heat a little oil in a nonstick skillet, add a batch of tortilla wedges, and fry over medium heat until crisp. Repeat with the remaining wedges and transfer to a serving platter.

Cut each avocado in half around the pit. Twist apart, then remove the pit with a knife. Carefully peel off the skin and dice the flesh. Gently stir the avocado into the shrimp mixture.

Top each tortilla wedge with a small mound of the shrimp and avocado mixture. Finish with a little sour cream, garnish with a light sprinkling of chili powder, and serve at once while hot and crisp with lime wedges.

cook's tip

For speed, you can use crisp corn tortillas (tostadas) or nacho chips (not too salty) instead of the soft corn tortillas.

variation

Substitute diced mozzarella or mild fresh romano cheese for the shrimp and marinate for a few hours.

black bean nachos

serves 4

15 minutes, plus 8 hours
soaking (optional)

1 hour 45 minutes

8 oz/225 g dried black beans, or
 canned black beans, drained
1½–2 cups grated cheese, such as
 Cheddar, fontina, romano, Asiago,
 or a combination
about ¼ tsp cumin seeds or ground
 cumin
about 4 tbsp sour cream

thinly sliced pickled jalapeño chiles
 (optional)
1 tbsp chopped fresh cilantro
handful of shredded lettuce
tortilla chips, to serve

*Packed with authentic
Mexican flavors, this tasty
black bean and cheese dip is
fun to eat and will get any
meal off to a good start! As an
added bonus, it takes mere
minutes to put together.*

variation

*To add a meaty flavor, spoon
chopped and browned chorizo
on top of the beans before
sprinkling over the cheese and
baking—the combination is
excellent. Finely chopped leftover
cooked meat can also be added
in this way.*

If using dried black beans, soak the beans overnight, then drain. Put into a pan, cover with water, and bring to a boil. Boil for 10 minutes, then reduce the heat and simmer for 1½ hours, or until tender. Drain well.

Preheat the oven to 375°F/190°C. Spread the beans in a shallow oven-proof dish, then scatter the cheese over the top. Sprinkle with cumin to taste.

Bake in the preheated oven for 10–15 minutes, or until the beans are cooked through and the cheese is bubbly and melted.

Remove from the oven and spoon the sour cream on top. Add the chiles, if using, and sprinkle with cilantro and lettuce.

Arrange the tortilla chips around the beans, placing them in the mixture. Serve the nachos at once.

refried **bean nachos**

serves 6–8

15 minutes

15 minutes

14 oz/400 g Refried Beans (see page 145) or canned
14 oz/400 g canned pinto beans, drained
large pinch of ground cumin
large pinch of mild chili powder
6 oz/175 g tortilla chips
2 cups grated cheese, such as Cheddar
salsa of your choice

1 avocado, pitted, peeled, diced, and tossed with lime juice
1/2 small onion or 3–5 scallions, chopped
2 ripe tomatoes, diced
handful of shredded lettuce
3–4 tbsp chopped fresh cilantro
sour cream, to serve

A Mexican classic, refried beans and tortilla chips are topped with luscious melted cheese, salsa, and assorted toppings, to make an irresistible dip. Perfect for an informal gathering!

variation

Replace the sour cream with strained plain yogurt as an alternative.

Preheat the oven to 400°F/200°C. Place the beans in a pan with the cumin and chili powder. Add enough water to make a thick soup-like consistency, stirring gently so that the beans do not lose their texture.

Heat the bean mixture over medium heat until hot, then reduce the heat and keep the mixture warm while you prepare the rest of the dish.

Arrange half the tortilla chips in the bottom of a flameproof casserole or gratin dish and cover with the bean mixture. Sprinkle with the cheese and bake in the preheated oven for 10 minutes, or until the cheese melts. Alternatively, place the casserole under a preheated hot broiler and broil for 5–7 minutes, or until the cheese melts and lightly sizzles in places.

Arrange on top of the melted cheese the salsa, avocado, onion, tomatoes, lettuce, and cilantro. Surround with the remaining tortilla chips and serve immediately with sour cream.

sincronizadas

serves 6

10 minutes

15 minutes

vegetable oil, for oiling
about 10 flour tortillas
about 4½ cups grated cheese
8 oz/225 g cooked ham, diced

salsa of your choice
sour cream sprinkled with chopped
  fresh herbs, to serve

Once you've tried this Mexican version of a toasted ham and cheese sandwich, you'll never look back! Serve with a tangy salsa and Mexican beer to complete the snack.

Lightly oil a nonstick skillet. Off the heat, place one tortilla in the skillet and top with a layer of cheese and ham. Generously spread salsa over another tortilla and place, salsa-side down, on top of the cheese and ham tortilla in the skillet.

Place over medium heat and cook until the cheese is melted and the bottom of the tortilla is golden brown.

Place a heatproof plate, upside-down, on top of the skillet. Taking care to protect your hands, hold the plate firmly in place and carefully invert the skillet to turn the "sandwich" out on to the plate.

Slide the "sandwich" back into the skillet and cook until the underside of the tortilla is golden brown.

Remove from the skillet and serve, cut into wedges, with sour cream sprinkled with herbs. Repeat with the remaining ingredients.

cook's tip

Protect your hands with oven gloves when turning the tortillas out on to the plate.

variation

For a vegetarian version, cook 8 oz/225 g thinly sliced mushrooms in a little olive oil with a crushed garlic clove and use instead of the ham. Alternatively, lightly fry finely chopped garlic in a little oil, then add rinsed spinach leaves and cook until wilted; chop and substitute for the ham.

tortas

serves 4

10 minutes

10 minutes

4 crusty rolls, such as French rolls or bocadillos

melted butter or olive oil, for brushing

8 oz/225 g Refried Beans (see page 145) or canned

12 oz/350 g shredded cooked chicken, browned chorizo sausage pieces, sliced ham, and cheese or any leftover cooked meat you have to hand

1 ripe tomato, sliced or diced

1 small onion, finely chopped

2 tbsp chopped fresh cilantro

1 avocado, pitted, peeled, sliced, and tossed with lime juice

4–6 tbsp sour cream or strained plain yogurt

salsa of your choice

handful of shredded lettuce

Throughout Mexico you'll find street vendors selling these substantial Mexican rolls. Filled with all sorts of ingredients, they are "muy delicioso"! Make your own and vary the filling as you wish.

variation

Add any Mexican sauce, such as Chile Verde (see page 205), to the meat filling to vary the flavor.

Cut the rolls in half and, using your fingers, remove a little of the crumb to make space for the filling.

Brush the outside and inside of the rolls with butter and toast, on both sides, in a hot grill pan or skillet for a few minutes until crisp. Alternatively, preheat the oven to 400°F/200°C and bake until lightly toasted.

Meanwhile, place the beans in a pan with a tiny amount of water and heat through gently.

When the rolls are heated, spread one half of each roll generously with the beans, then top with a layer of cooked meat. Top with tomato, onion, cilantro, and avocado.

Generously spread sour cream on to the other side of each roll. Drizzle the salsa over the filling, add a little shredded lettuce, then sandwich the two sides of each roll together; press tightly. Serve immediately.

molletes

serves 4

15 minutes

40 minutes

4 bread rolls

1 tbsp vegetable oil, plus extra for brushing

14 oz/400 g Refried Beans (see page 145) or canned

1 onion, chopped

3 garlic cloves, chopped

3 bacon strips, cut into small pieces, or about 3 oz/85 g chorizo sausage, diced

8 oz/225 g diced fresh or canned tomatoes

¼–½ tsp ground cumin

2¼ cups grated cheese

cabbage salad

½ cabbage, thinly sliced

2 tbsp sliced pickled jalapeño chiles

1 tbsp extra-virgin olive oil

3 tbsp cider vinegar

¼ tsp dried oregano

salt and pepper

Molletes are crusty rolls stuffed with hot beans and melted cheese, then garnished with a tangy hot salsa. In this version, a spicy shredded cabbage salad adds extra crunch to the snacks.

Preheat the oven to 400°F/200°C. Cut the rolls in half and remove a little of the crumb to make space for the filling.

To make the salad, combine the cabbage with the chiles, olive oil, and vinegar in a bowl. Add the oregano and salt and pepper to taste. Set aside.

Brush the rolls all over with vegetable oil. Arrange on a cookie sheet and bake in the preheated oven for 10–15 minutes, or until the rolls are crisp and light golden.

Meanwhile, place the beans in a pan and heat through gently with enough water to thin them to a smooth paste.

Heat the 1 tablespoon of vegetable oil in a skillet. Add the onion, garlic, and bacon or chorizo and cook until the bacon or chorizo is browned and the onion is softened. Add the tomatoes and simmer, stirring, until they break down to form a thick sauce.

Add the warmed beans to the skillet and stir to combine with the mixture. Stir in the cumin to taste. Set aside.

Remove the rolls from the oven; keep the oven on. Fill the rolls with the warm bean mixture, then top with the cheese and close up tightly. Return to the cookie sheet and heat through in the oven until the cheese melts.

Open the rolls up and spoon in a little of the salad. Serve immediately.

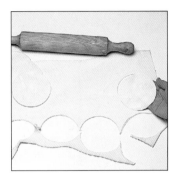

spicy-sweet meat empanadas

 serves 4

 15 minutes

 15–25 minutes

12 oz/350 g ready-made puff pastry
all-purpose flour, for dusting
1 quantity Spicy Beef Filling (see page 199)
1 egg yolk, beaten with 1–2 tbsp water

to serve
green olives
mixed chiles

This is a great make-ahead appetizer as it can be frozen for a month, then just popped into the oven at the last moment—it will still taste marvelous!

Preheat the oven to 375°F/190°C. Roll out the pie dough into a thin layer on a lightly floured counter. Using a 6-inch/15-cm cookie cutter, cut the dough into 8 rounds.

Place a tablespoon or two of the filling in the center of one round.

Brush the edge of the dough with beaten egg, then fold in half and press the edges together to seal.

Press the tines of a fork along the sealed edges of the dough to make the seal more secure. Prick the top of the empanada with the fork, then place on a cookie sheet. Brush with beaten egg. Repeat this process with the remaining dough rounds and filling.

Bake in the preheated oven for 15–25 minutes, or until a light golden brown on the outside and hot in the middle.

Serve immediately, hot and sizzling from the oven, accompanied by a bowl of olives and chiles.

variation

For chicken empanadas, replace the Spicy Beef Filling with diced cooked chicken, flavored with some mild chili sauce.

For vegetarian empanadas, replace the filling with a mixture of diced Swiss or Cheddar cheese, chopped onion, fresh cilantro, cumin seeds, and sliced pimiento-stuffed green olives. Fill and bake as described.

masa tartlets with
beans & avocado

serves 4

35 minutes

30 minutes

8–10 tbsp masa harina
3 tbsp all-purpose flour
pinch of baking powder
1 cup warm water
vegetable oil, for frying
8 oz/225 g canned pinto beans or refried beans, warmed
1 avocado, pitted, peeled, sliced, and tossed with lime juice

3 oz/85 g queso fresco, fresh cream cheese, or crumbled feta cheese
salsa of your choice
2 scallions, thinly sliced

to garnish
fresh flatleaf parsley sprigs
lemon wedges

Packed with Mexican flavors, these little golden tartlets make a colorful start to a meal or a tasty light lunch when served with mixed salad greens.

Mix the masa harina with the flour and baking powder in a bowl, then mix in enough warm water to make a firm yet moist dough.

Pinch off about a walnut-size piece of dough and, using your fingers, shape into a tiny tartlet shape, pressing and pinching to make it as thin as possible without falling apart. Repeat with the remaining dough.

Heat a layer of oil in a deep skillet until it is smoking. Add a batch of tartlets to the hot oil and fry, spooning the hot fat into the center of the tartlets and turning once, until golden on all sides.

Using a slotted spoon, remove the tartlets from the hot oil and drain on paper towels. Place on a cookie sheet and keep warm in the oven on low temperature while cooking the remaining tartlets.

Fill each tartlet shell with the warmed beans, avocado, cheese, salsa, and scallions. Garnish with parsley and lemon wedges and serve at once.

salads, side dishes & sauces

Salads of crisp, raw vegetables and fruits, often eaten piled on top of richer savory cooked dishes, such as enchiladas or grilled food, are full of fresh flavor and rich with vitamins, too. Pomegranate, papaya, and tangy citrus fruits are combined with avocado or red bell peppers to stunning effect.

For heartier salads, Steak, Avocado & Bean Salad (see page 71) is a substantial dish, while summer squash and chorizo sausage, two popular ingredients in Mexico, make the basis for a great lunchtime snack.

For a delicious side dish, try a gratin of potatoes lavished with mild red chili sauce, layered with goat cheese and baked until lightly crusty. Or try fragrant Roasted Green Chiles in Cumin-Garlic Cream (see page 81)—a classic accompaniment to all sorts of entrées.

Sauces for topping meat and fish or for filling tortillas are on offer here, too. Quick Tomato Sauce (see page 83) can be used for many dishes, while Hot Sauce of Dried Chiles (see page 89) will add a fieriness that is the very essence of Mexican cuisine. Mole Poblano (see page 91), the classic sauce of chiles and chocolate, is not to be missed.

papaya, avocado &
red bell pepper salad

serves 4–6

20 minutes

7 oz/200 g mixed salad greens

2–3 scallions, chopped

3–4 tbsp chopped fresh cilantro

1 small papaya

2 red bell peppers

1 avocado

1 tbsp lime juice

3–4 tbsp pumpkin seeds, preferably toasted (optional)

dressing

juice of 1 lime

large pinch of paprika

large pinch of ground cumin

large pinch of sugar

1 garlic clove, finely chopped

4 tbsp extra-virgin olive oil

salt

dash of white wine vinegar (optional)

This colorful and refreshing salad, with its sweet and spicy flavors, is the perfect foil to a meaty main dish, and is particularly good with barbecued foods.

Combine the salad greens with the scallions and cilantro in a bowl. Mix well, then transfer the salad to a large serving dish.

Cut the papaya in half and scoop out the seeds with a spoon. Cut into quarters, remove the peel, and slice the flesh. Arrange on top of the salad greens. Cut the bell peppers in half, remove the cores and seeds, then thinly slice. Add the bell peppers to the salad greens.

Cut the avocado in half around the pit. Twist apart, then remove the pit with a knife. Carefully peel off the skin, dice the flesh, and toss in lime juice to prevent discoloration. Add to the other salad ingredients.

To make the dressing, whisk the lime juice, paprika, cumin, sugar, garlic, and oil together in a small bowl. Season to taste with salt.

Pour the dressing over the salad and toss lightly, adding a dash of wine vinegar if a flavor with more "bite" is preferred. Sprinkle with pumpkin seeds, if using.

green bean salad
with feta cheese

serves 4

10 minutes

5 minutes

12 oz/350 g green beans

1 red onion, chopped

3–4 tbsp chopped fresh cilantro

2 radishes, thinly sliced

2¾ oz/75 g feta cheese (drained weight), crumbled

1 tsp chopped fresh oregano, plus extra leaves to garnish (optional), or ½ tsp dried

pepper

2 tbsp red wine or fruit vinegar

⅓ cup extra-virgin olive oil

3 ripe tomatoes, cut into wedges

This fresh-tasting salad is flavored with fresh cilantro, a herb widely used in Mexican cooking.

variation

This recipe is also delicious made with nopales, or edible cactus, which is used as a vegetable in Mexican cooking. It is available in specialty markets in cans or jars. Simply drain the cactus, then slice and use instead of the green beans, missing out the first step. When using cactus, replace the feta cheese with 1–2 chopped hard-cooked eggs.

Bring about 2 inches/5 cm of water to a boil in the bottom of a steamer. Add the beans to the top part of the steamer, cover, and steam for 5 minutes, or until just tender.

Place the beans in a large bowl and add the onion, cilantro, radishes, and feta cheese.

Sprinkle the oregano over the salad, then season to taste with pepper. Mix the vinegar and oil together in a small bowl and pour over the salad. Toss gently to mix well.

Transfer to a serving platter, surround with the tomato wedges, and serve at once, or cover and chill until ready to serve.

citrus salad with pomegranate

serves 4

20 minutes

–

1 large pomegranate
1 grapefruit
2 sweet oranges
finely grated rind of ½ lime
1–2 garlic cloves, finely chopped
3 tbsp red wine vinegar
juice of 2 limes
½ tsp sugar

¼ tsp dry mustard
salt and pepper
4–5 tbsp extra-virgin olive oil
1 head red leafy lettuce, such as oak
  leaf, washed and dried
1 avocado, pitted, peeled, diced, and
  tossed with a little lime juice
½ red onion, thinly sliced, to garnish

A salad like this reveals how much Mexico and the Mediterranean share in terms of sunny flavors and ingredients.

Cut the pomegranate into quarters, then press back the outer skin to push out the seeds into a bowl.

Using a sharp knife, cut a slice off the top and bottom of the grapefruit, then remove the peel and pith, cutting downward. Cut out the segments from between the membranes, then add to the pomegranate.

Finely grate the rind of half an orange and set aside. Using a sharp knife, cut a slice off the top and bottom of both oranges, then remove the peel and pith, cutting downward and taking care to retain the shape of the oranges. Slice horizontally into slices, then cut into quarters. Add the oranges to the pomegranate and grapefruit and stir to mix well.

Combine the reserved orange rind with the lime rind, garlic, vinegar, lime juice, sugar, and mustard in a small nonmetallic bowl. Season to taste with salt and pepper, then whisk in the oil.

Place the lettuce leaves in a serving bowl, then top with the fruit mixture and the avocado. Pour over the dressing and toss gently. Garnish with the onion rings and serve at once.

zucchini with
green chile vinaigrette

serves 4

30 minutes

10 minutes

1 large fresh mild green chile or a combination of 1 green bell pepper and ½–1 fresh green chile

4 zucchini, sliced

2–3 garlic cloves, finely chopped

pinch of sugar

¼ tsp ground cumin

2 tbsp white wine vinegar

4 tbsp extra-virgin olive oil

2–3 tbsp chopped fresh cilantro

salt and pepper

4 ripe tomatoes, diced or sliced

tortilla chips, to serve (optional)

Lightly cooked zucchini are mixed with ripe, juicy tomatoes and dressed with a chile vinaigrette to create a perfect side salad for a summer lunch or supper.

Roast the chile, or the combination of the green bell pepper and chile, in an unoiled heavy-bottomed skillet or under a preheated hot broiler until the skin is charred. Place in a plastic bag, twist to seal well, and let stand for 20 minutes.

Peel the skin from the chile and bell pepper, if using, then remove the seeds and slice the flesh. Set aside.

Bring about 2 inches/5 cm of water to a boil in the bottom of a steamer. Add the zucchini to the top part of the steamer, cover, and steam for 5 minutes, or until just tender.

Meanwhile, thoroughly combine the garlic, sugar, cumin, vinegar, oil, and cilantro in a bowl. Stir in the chile and bell pepper, if using, then season to taste with salt and pepper.

Arrange the zucchini and tomatoes in a serving bowl or on a platter and spoon over the chile dressing. Toss gently and serve with tortilla chips, if wished.

variation
Add 8 oz/225 g cooked, shelled shrimp to the zucchini and tomatoes before coating with the dressing.

steak, avocado & bean salad

serves 4

15 minutes,
plus 30 minutes marinating

6 minutes

12 oz/350 g tender steak, such as
 sirloin

4 garlic cloves, chopped

juice of 1 lime

4 tbsp extra-virgin olive oil

salt and pepper

1 tbsp white or red wine vinegar

1/4 tsp mild chili powder

1/4 tsp ground cumin

1/2 tsp paprika

pinch of sugar (optional)

5 scallions, thinly sliced

about 7 oz/200 g crisp lettuce leaves,
 such as romaine, or mixed fresh
 herb leaves

8 oz/225 g canned corn kernels,
 drained

14 oz/400 g canned pinto, black, or
 red kidney beans, drained

1 avocado, pitted, peeled, sliced, and
 tossed with a little lime juice

2 ripe tomatoes, diced

1/4 fresh green or red chile, chopped

3 tbsp chopped fresh cilantro

generous handful of crisp tortilla
 chips, broken into pieces

*The Californian influence
on Mexican food is evident in
this big, hearty salad. Packed
with delicious ingredients, this
fantastic dish is a meal in itself.*

Place the steak in a nonmetallic dish with the garlic and half the lime juice and oil. Season to taste with salt and pepper, cover, and let marinate for 30 minutes.

To make the dressing, combine the remaining lime juice and oil with the vinegar, chili powder, cumin, and paprika in a small nonmetallic bowl. Add the sugar, if using, then set aside.

Pan-fry the steak, or cook under a preheated very hot broiler, until browned on the outside and cooked to your liking in the middle. Transfer to a board, cut into strips, and reserve; keep warm or let cool.

Toss the scallions with the lettuce and arrange on a serving platter. Pour half the dressing over the leaves, then arrange the corn, beans, avocado, and tomatoes over the top. Sprinkle with the chile and cilantro.

Arrange the steak and the tortilla chips on top, pour over the rest of the dressing, and serve at once.

zucchini & summer
squash with chorizo

serves 4

10 minutes

10 minutes

2 zucchini, thinly sliced
2 yellow summer squash, thinly sliced
salt and pepper
2 fresh chorizo sausages, diced
   or sliced
3 garlic cloves, finely chopped

juice of 1/2–1 lime
1–2 tbsp chopped fresh cilantro

The spicy richness of chorizo marries well with zucchini and squash, giving them a real flavor lift.

Cook the zucchini and summer squash in a pan of boiling salted water for 3–4 minutes, or until they are just tender. Drain well.

Brown the chorizo in a heavy-bottomed skillet, stirring with a spoon to break up into pieces. Pour off any excess fat from the browned chorizo, then add the garlic and blanched zucchini and summer squash. Cook for a few minutes, stirring gently, to combine the flavors.

Stir in the lime juice to taste. Season to taste with salt and pepper and serve at once sprinkled with chopped cilantro.

cook's tip

Mild in flavor and ideal for combining with spicy meats, squash is a favorite Mexican vegetable. If wished, this dish can be prepared with squash only— yellow pattypans would be ideal.

variation

For variety, why not use the rather more exotic squash known as chayote or cho-cho, which is indigenous to Mexico. This is pear-shaped and is usually pale green, with a corrugated skin. To prepare, simply peel and slice, then blanch as for the zucchini, but cooking for a few minutes longer. Use with yellow-colored zucchini for visual appeal.

summer squash with green chiles & corn

serves 4–6

10 minutes

10 minutes

2 corn cobs

2 small zucchini or other green summer squash, such as pattypans, cubed or sliced

2 small yellow summer squash, cubed or sliced

2 tbsp butter

3 garlic cloves, finely chopped

3–4 large ripe flavorful tomatoes, diced

several pinches of mild chili powder

several pinches of ground cumin

½ fresh green chile, such as jalapeño, seeded and chopped

pinch of sugar

salt and pepper

Garlicky butter and a hint of chili flavor this summertime vegetable pot of squash and corn. Serve alongside almost any meaty main course; good, too, with fajitas.

variation

Any leftovers will make a good base for a lovely summer soup. Simply thin with lots of stock and freshen up with chopped fresh herbs.

Bring about 2 inches/5 cm of water to a boil in the bottom of a steamer. Add the corn, zucchini, and summer squash to the top part of the steamer, cover, and steam for about 3 minutes, depending on their maturity and freshness. Alternatively, blanch in a pan of boiling salted water for 3 minutes, then drain. Set aside until cool enough to handle.

Using a large knife, slice the kernels off the cobs and set aside.

Melt the butter in a heavy-bottomed skillet. Add the garlic and cook for 1 minute to soften. Add the tomatoes, chili powder, cumin, chile, and sugar. Season to taste with salt and pepper and cook for a few minutes, or until the flavors have mingled.

Add the corn kernels, zucchini, and squash. Cook for 2 minutes, stirring, to warm through. Serve at once.

potatoes in
green sauce

serves 6

5 minutes

25 minutes

2 lb 4 oz/1 kg small waxy potatoes, peeled

salt

1 onion, halved and unpeeled

8 garlic cloves, unpeeled

1 fresh green chile

8 tomatillos, outer husks removed, or small tart tomatoes

1 cup chicken, meat, or vegetable stock, preferably homemade

½ tsp ground cumin

1 fresh thyme sprig or generous pinch of dried thyme

1 fresh oregano sprig or generous pinch of dried oregano

2 tbsp vegetable or virgin olive oil

1 zucchini, coarsely chopped

1 bunch fresh cilantro, chopped

Earthy potatoes, served in a tangy spicy tomatillo sauce and topped with scallions and sour cream, are delicious either as a side dish with simmered or braised meat, or as a vegetarian entrée.

Place the potatoes in a pan of salted water. Bring to a boil and cook for 15 minutes, or until almost tender. Do not overcook them. Drain and set aside.

Lightly char the onion, garlic, chile, and tomatillos or tomatoes in an unoiled heavy-bottomed skillet. Set aside. When cool enough to handle, peel and chop the onion, garlic, and chile; chop the tomatillos or tomatoes. Place in a food processor or blender with half the stock and process to form a purée. Add the cumin, thyme, and oregano and stir well to combine.

Heat the oil in the heavy-bottomed skillet. Add the purée and cook for 5 minutes, stirring, to reduce slightly and concentrate the flavors.

Add the potatoes and zucchini to the purée and pour in the rest of the stock. Add about half the cilantro and cook for an additional 5 minutes, or until the zucchini are tender.

Transfer to a serving bowl and serve sprinkled with the remaining chopped cilantro to garnish.

potatoes with
chipotle cream

serves 4

10 minutes

35 minutes

2 lb 12 oz/1.25 kg baking potatoes, peeled and cut into chunks

pinch of salt

pinch of sugar

generous ¾ cup sour cream

½ cup vegetable or chicken stock

3 garlic cloves, finely chopped

few shakes of bottled chipotle salsa or ½ dried chipotle, reconstituted (see page 100), seeded, and thinly sliced

8 oz/225 g goat cheese, sliced

6 oz/175 g mozzarella or Cheddar cheese, grated

1¾ oz/50 g Parmesan or romano cheese, grated

This makes a luscious side dish to serve with meat, or a satisfying vegetarian entrée. Goat cheese is a traditional food of Mexico, and is enjoying great renewed popularity.

Preheat the oven to 350°F/180°C. Place the potatoes in a pan of water with the salt and sugar. Bring to a boil and cook for 10 minutes, or until they are half cooked.

Combine the sour cream with the stock, garlic, and the chipotle salsa in a bowl.

Arrange half the potatoes in a flameproof casserole. Pour half the sour cream sauce over the potatoes and cover with the goat cheese slices. Top with the remaining potatoes and the sauce.

Sprinkle with the grated mozzarella or Cheddar cheese, then with either the grated Parmesan or romano cheese.

Bake in the oven for 30 minutes, or until the potatoes are tender and the cheese topping is lightly golden and crisp in places. Serve at once.

roasted green chiles in cumin-garlic cream

serves 4–6

15 minutes,
plus 20 minutes standing

25 minutes

4 large fresh mild green chiles, such as Anaheim or poblano, or a combination of 4 green bell peppers and 2 jalapeño chiles

2 tbsp butter

1 onion, finely chopped

3 garlic cloves, finely chopped

1/4 tsp ground cumin

salt and pepper

1 cup light cream

1 cup chicken or vegetable stock

1 lime, halved, to serve

Roasted mild green chiles are delicious simmered with cumin-scented cream. It's important not to make this too hot, otherwise the fragrant aromas will be overpowered.

variation

Add an equal amount of corn with the chiles—they add a delicious sweetness to the dish.

Roast the mild chiles, or the combination of bell peppers and jalapeño chiles, in an unoiled heavy-bottomed skillet or under a preheated hot broiler until the skins are charred. Place in a plastic bag, twist to seal well, and let stand for 20 minutes.

Peel the skin from the chiles and bell peppers, if using, and remove the seeds and slice the flesh. Set aside.

Melt the butter in a large skillet. Add the onion and garlic and cook for 3 minutes, or until softened. Sprinkle with the cumin and season to taste with salt and pepper.

Stir in the sliced chiles and bell peppers, if using, and pour in the cream and stock. Cook over medium heat, stirring, until the liquid reduces in volume and forms a richly flavored sauce.

Transfer to a serving dish and serve warm, squeezing over lime juice at the last minute.

quick tomato sauce

serves 4–6

5–10 minutes

10 minutes

2 tbsp vegetable or olive oil

1 onion, thinly sliced

5 garlic cloves, thinly sliced

14 oz/400 g canned tomatoes, diced, plus their juices, or 1 lb 5 oz/600 g fresh diced tomatoes

several shakes of mild chili powder

1 1/2 cups vegetable or chicken stock

salt and pepper

pinch of sugar (optional)

Simple to make, this versatile sauce is not only a great accompaniment for grilled meat and fish, but also invaluable for baked tortilla dishes and taco fillings.

Heat the oil in a large skillet. Add the onion and garlic and cook for 3 minutes, or until just softened, stirring constantly.

Add the tomatoes, chili powder to taste, and the stock. Cook over medium–high heat for 10 minutes, or until the tomatoes have reduced slightly and the flavor of the sauce is more concentrated.

Season the sauce to taste with salt, pepper, and sugar, if using. Serve the dish warm.

cook's tip

The sauce will keep covered in the refrigerator for up to 3 days.

If using fresh tomatoes for this sauce, make sure they are very ripe and flavorful. Peel and seed fresh tomatoes before dicing.

variation

For a hotter kick, add 1/2 teaspoon of finely chopped fresh chile with the onion.

hot tomato sauce

serves 4

5–10 minutes

–

2–3 fresh green chiles, such as
  jalapeño or serrano

8 oz/225 g canned chopped tomatoes

1 scallion, thinly sliced

2 garlic cloves, chopped

2–3 tbsp cider vinegar

1/4–1/3 cup water

large pinch of dried oregano

large pinch of ground cumin

large pinch of sugar

large pinch of salt

This tangy sauce is excellent with crispy tortillas and tostadas, or with broiled or fried fish.

cook's tip

If you have sensitive skin, it may be advisable to wear rubber gloves when preparing fresh chiles, as the oil in the seeds and flesh can cause irritation. Make sure that you do not touch your eyes when handling cut chiles.

Slice the chiles open, remove the seeds if wished, then chop the chiles.

Place the chiles in a food processor or blender with the tomatoes, scallion, garlic, cider vinegar, water, oregano, cumin, sugar, and salt. Process until smooth.

Adjust the seasoning, cover, and chill until ready to serve. The sauce will keep for up to 1 week, covered, in the refrigerator.

mild red chili sauce

Makes about 1½ cups

10 minutes,
plus 20 minutes cooling

15–20 minutes

5 large fresh mild chiles, such as New Mexico or ancho

2 cups vegetable or chicken stock

1 tbsp masa harina or 1 crumbled corn tortilla, puréed with enough water to make a thin paste

large pinch of ground cumin

1–2 garlic cloves, finely chopped

juice of 1 lime

salt (optional)

This milder sauce is ideal for enchiladas and stewed meat. Keep some stashed in your freezer at all times for an instant hit of Mexico!

Using metal tongs, roast each chile over an open flame for a few seconds until the color darkens on all sides. Alternatively, place the chiles under a preheated hot broiler, turning them frequently.

Place the chiles in a heatproof bowl and pour boiling water over them. Cover and let the chiles cool.

Meanwhile, place the stock in a pan and bring to a simmer.

When the chiles have cooled and are swelled up and softened, remove from the water with a slotted spoon. Remove the seeds from the chiles, then cut or tear the flesh into pieces and place in a food processor or blender. Process to form a purée, then mix in the hot stock.

Place the chile and stock mixture in a pan. Add the masa harina or puréed tortilla, cumin, garlic, and lime juice. Bring to a boil and cook for a few minutes, stirring, until the sauce has thickened. Add salt to taste, if necessary, and serve.

hot sauce of dried chiles

 makes about 1 cup

 5 minutes, plus 30 minutes standing

 10 minutes

10 dried arbol chiles, stalks removed (see Cook's Tip)

1 cup cider or white wine vinegar

1/2 tsp salt

Perfect for adding a splash of authentic hot Mexican flavor to a dish, this sauce will prove to be a handy standby.

cook's tip

The sauce can be bottled by pouring into sterilized jars and treating it as you would any long-keeping jam, jelly, or preserve.

Arbol are dried long hot red chiles, with a dusty heat that is reminiscent of the Mexican desert. If arbol chiles are not available, use any hot dried chile, or chili flakes, such as cayenne.

Place the chiles in a mortar and crush finely with a pestle.

Place the vinegar in a pan and add the crushed chiles and salt. Stir to combine, then bring the liquid to a boil.

Remove the pan from the heat and let cool completely to allow the flavors to infuse. Pour into a bowl and serve. The sauce will keep for up to 1 month, covered, in the refrigerator.

mole poblano

serves 8–10

20 minutes,
plus 1 hour standing

15 minutes

3 dried mulato chiles

3 mild dried ancho chiles

5–6 dried New Mexico or California chiles

1 onion, chopped

5 garlic cloves, chopped

1 lb/450 g ripe tomatoes

2 tortillas, preferably stale, cut into small pieces

pinch of cloves

pinch of fennel seeds

1/8 tsp each ground cinnamon, coriander, and cumin

3 tbsp lightly toasted sesame seeds or tahini

3 tbsp slivered or coarsely ground blanched almonds

2 tbsp raisins

1 tbsp peanut butter (optional)

2 cups chicken stock

3–4 tbsp grated semisweet chocolate, plus extra to garnish

2 tbsp mild chili powder

3 tbsp vegetable oil

salt and pepper

about 1 tbsp lime juice

This great Mexican celebration dish, ladled out at village fiestas, birthday parties, baptisms, and weddings, is known for its unusual combination of chiles and chocolate.

Using metal tongs, roast each chile over an open flame for a few seconds until the color darkens on all sides. Alternatively, roast in an unoiled skillet over medium heat for 30 seconds, turning constantly.

Place the roasted chiles in a heatproof bowl or a pan and pour over enough boiling water to cover. Cover with a lid and let soften for at least 1 hour or overnight. Once or twice, lift the lid and rearrange the chiles so that they soak evenly.

Remove the softened chiles with a slotted spoon. Discard the stalks and seeds and cut the flesh into pieces. Place in a food processor or blender.

Add the onion, garlic, tomatoes, tortillas, cloves, fennel seeds, cinnamon, coriander, cumin, sesame seeds, almonds, raisins, and peanut butter, if using, then process to combine. With the motor running, add enough stock through the feed tube to make a smooth paste. Stir in the remaining stock, chocolate, and chili powder.

Heat the oil in a heavy-bottomed pan until it is smoking, then pour in the mole mixture. It will splatter and pop as it hits the hot oil. Cook for 10 minutes, stirring occasionally to prevent it burning.

Season to taste with salt, pepper, and lime juice, garnish with a little grated chocolate, and serve.

mole verde

serves 4–6

15 minutes

15 minutes

2¼ cups toasted pumpkin seeds

4 cups chicken stock

several pinches of ground cloves

8–10 tomatillos, diced, or use
  1⅓ cups mild tomatillo salsa

½ onion, chopped

½ fresh green chile, seeded and
  diced

3 garlic cloves, chopped

½ tsp fresh thyme leaves

½ tsp fresh marjoram leaves

3 tbsp shortening or vegetable oil

3 bay leaves

4 tbsp chopped fresh cilantro

salt and pepper

fresh green chile slices, to garnish

Moles are purées and, depending on the ingredients, they vary in color from yellow and green to chocolate brown. This green mole is a specialty of Jalisco. Serve with warm corn tortillas or unfilled Tamales (see page 139).

variation

Mix up a tamale dough (see page 139) and poach in the mole as dumplings, making a filling snack.

Grind the toasted pumpkin seeds in a food processor. Add half the stock, the cloves, tomatillos, onion, chile, garlic, thyme, and marjoram and blend to a purée.

Heat the shortening in a heavy-bottomed skillet and add the puréed pumpkin seed mixture and the bay leaves. Cook over medium–high heat for 5 minutes, or until the mixture begins to thicken.

Remove the skillet from the heat and add the remaining stock and the cilantro. Return the skillet to the heat and cook until the sauce thickens, then remove from the heat.

Remove the bay leaves and place the sauce in a food processor or blender and process until completely smooth. Add salt and pepper to taste.

Transfer to a serving bowl, garnish with chile slices, and serve.

salsa, tortillas, beans & rice

Salsas appear on every table in every corner of Mexico. They are what add interest to often simple fare. What's more, they are delicious and good for you, too, as long as you don't burn your tongue! In this chapter you'll find the full range, from sizzling Salsa Verde (see page 103) to powerful and smoky Chipotle Salsa (see page 99) and cooling Fresh Pineapple Salsa (see page 107).

Tortillas are not only the bread of Mexico, they are also its knives and forks: break off a piece of tortilla, wrap it up in whatever you are eating, and you have an instant taco, no eating utensils needed. The variety of dishes made with tortillas in this chapter range from fish-filled tacos and tostadas topped with chicken and salsa, to burritos filled with lamb and black beans. In Mexico, beans and rice are eaten every day for nearly every meal. Discover how to make Mexico's famous dish of Refried Beans (see page 145), and learn the secret of Green Rice (see page 154), flavored with onions, garlic, chile, and cilantro.

Salsas, dishes of tortillas, beans, and rice are the very soul of Mexico.

two classic salsas

serves 4–6

5 minutes

–

jalapeño salsa

1 onion, finely chopped

2–3 garlic cloves, finely chopped

4–6 tbsp coarsely chopped pickled jalapeño chiles

juice of 1/2 lemon

about 1/4 tsp ground cumin

salt

salsa cruda

6–8 ripe tomatoes, finely chopped

about 1/3 cup tomato juice

3–4 garlic cloves, finely chopped

1/2–1 bunch fresh cilantro leaves, coarsely chopped

pinch of sugar

3–4 fresh green chiles, such as jalapeño or serrano, seeded and finely chopped

1/2–1 tsp ground cumin

3–4 scallions, finely chopped

salt

A Mexican meal is not complete without an accompanying salsa. These two traditional salsas are ideal for seasoning any dish, from filled tortillas to grilled meat— they add a spicy hotness that is the very essence of Mexican cooking.

To make the jalapeño salsa, place the onion in a nonmetallic bowl with the garlic, chiles, lemon juice, and cumin. Season to taste with salt and stir together. Cover and chill until required.

To make a chunky-textured salsa cruda, stir all the ingredients together in a nonmetallic bowl, adding salt to taste. Cover and chill until required.

To make a smoother-textured salsa, process the ingredients in a food processor or blender. Cover and chill until required.

cook's tip

You can vary the amount of garlic, chiles, and ground spices according to taste, but make sure the salsa has quite a "kick", otherwise it will not be effective.

variation

For the salsa cruda, substitute finely chopped orange segments and seeded diced cucumber for the tomatoes to add a fresh, fruity taste.

chipotle salsa

makes about 2 cups

5 minutes

–

1 lb/450 g ripe juicy tomatoes, diced

3–5 garlic cloves, finely chopped

1/2 bunch fresh cilantro leaves, coarsely chopped

1 small onion, chopped

1–2 tsp adobo marinade from canned chipotle chiles

1/2–1 tsp sugar

lime juice, to taste

salt

pinch of ground cinnamon (optional)

pinch of ground allspice (optional)

pinch of ground cumin (optional)

Chipotles are the smoked jalapeño chile sold either dried or in cans, packed in a spicy flavorful marinade called odobo. Here the marinade from the canned version is used to perk up a simple fresh tomato salsa.

cook's tip

To simplify preparation, the fresh tomatoes can be replaced with 14 oz/400 g canned chopped tomatoes.

Place the tomatoes, garlic, and cilantro in a food processor or blender.

Process the mixture until smooth, then add the onion, adobo marinade, and sugar.

Squeeze in lime juice to taste. Season to taste with salt, then add the cinnamon, allspice, and cumin, if using.

Serve at once, or cover and chill until ready to serve, although the salsa is at its best when served freshly made.

cooked chipotle salsa

makes about 2 cups

15 minutes

10 minutes

3 dried chipotle chiles
1 onion, finely chopped
14 oz/400 g canned tomatoes,
    including their juices
2–3 tbsp dark brown sugar
2–3 garlic cloves, finely chopped
pinch of ground cinnamon

pinch of ground cloves' or allspice
large pinch of ground cumin
juice of 1/2 lemon
1 tbsp extra-virgin olive oil
salt
finely pared strips of lemon rind,
    to garnish

This rich, tomato-red chipotle salsa is sweet and piquant, delicious with anything barbecued, or dabbed into a taco or burrito.

cook's tip

This salsa freezes extremely well. Freeze in an ice-cube tray, then pop the cubes out and store in a plastic bag, ready to use for individual portions.

Place the chiles in a pan with enough water to cover. Protecting your face against fumes and making sure that the kitchen is well ventilated, bring the chiles and water to a boil. Cook for 5 minutes, then remove the pan from the heat, cover, and let stand until softened.

Remove the chiles from the water with a slotted spoon. Cut away and discard the stalk and seeds, then either scrape the flesh from the skins or chop up the whole chiles.

Place the onion in a pan with the tomatoes and sugar and cook over medium heat, stirring, until thickened.

Remove the pan from the heat and add the garlic, cinnamon, cloves, cumin, lemon juice, oil, and prepared chipotle chiles. Season to taste with salt and let cool. Serve garnished with lemon rind.

hot mexican salsas

serves 4–6

10 minutes

5 minutes

tropical fruit salsa

½ sweet ripe pineapple, peeled, cored, and diced

1 mango or papaya, pitted or seeded, peeled, and diced

½–1 fresh green chile, such as jalapeño or serrano, seeded and chopped

½–1 fresh red chile, chopped

½ red onion, chopped

1 tbsp sugar

juice of 1 lime

3 tbsp chopped fresh mint

salt

scorched chile salsa

1 green bell pepper

2–3 fresh green chiles, such as jalapeño or serrano

2 garlic cloves, finely chopped

juice of ½ lime

1 tsp salt

2–3 tbsp extra-virgin olive oil or vegetable oil

large pinch of dried oregano

large pinch of ground cumin

salsa verde

1 lb/450 g canned tomatillos, drained and chopped, or tart fresh tomatoes, chopped

1–2 fresh green chiles, such as jalapeño or serrano, seeded and finely chopped

1 green bell pepper or large mild green chile, such as Anaheim or poblano, seeded and chopped

1 small onion, chopped

1 bunch fresh cilantro leaves, finely chopped

½ tsp ground cumin

salt

These salsas capture the inimitable tangy, spicy flavor of Mexico. Choose from a fresh minty fruit salsa, charred chile salsa, or a spicy "green" salsa.

To make the tropical fruit salsa, combine all the ingredients in a large non-metallic bowl, adding salt to taste. Cover the bowl and chill until required.

For the scorched chile salsa, char the bell pepper and chiles in an unoiled skillet. Cool, peel, seed, and chop. Mix with the garlic, lime juice, salt, and oil in a nonmetallic bowl. Top with oregano and cumin.

For the salsa verde, combine the ingredients in a nonmetallic bowl, adding salt to taste. If a smoother sauce is preferred, process the ingredients in a food processor until blended. Spoon into a bowl to serve.

salsa of marinated
chipotle chiles

serves 4–6

10 minutes

35–40 minutes

6 dried chipotle chiles

6 tbsp tomato ketchup

12 oz/350 g ripe tomatoes, diced

1 large onion, chopped

5 garlic cloves, chopped

2 tbsp cider vinegar

1¼ cups water

1 tbsp virgin olive oil

2 tbsp sugar, preferably molasses sugar

pinch of salt

¼ tsp ground allspice

¼ tsp ground cloves

¼ tsp ground cinnamon

¼ tsp ground cumin

pepper

3–4 tbsp lime juice or a combination of pineapple and lemon juice

Dried chipotle chiles make a spicy-sweet smoky relish, good for adding to tostadas, tacos, and any other tortilla dish.

Place the chiles in a pan with enough water to cover. Bring to a boil, taking care not to inhale the fumes given off as they can irritate your lungs. Simmer, covered, for 20 minutes, then remove the pan from the heat and let cool.

Remove the chiles from the water. Cut away and discard the stalks and seeds, then either scrape the flesh from the skins or chop up the whole chiles.

Place the tomato ketchup and tomatoes in a clean pan with the chiles, onion, garlic, vinegar, water, oil, sugar, salt, allspice, cloves, cinnamon, and cumin. Bring to a boil. Reduce the heat and simmer for 15 minutes, or until the mixture has thickened.

Season to taste with pepper, then stir in the fruit juice. Use as required.

fresh pineapple salsa

serves 4

15 minutes

–

½ ripe pineapple

juice of 1 lime or lemon

1 garlic clove, finely chopped

1 scallion, thinly sliced

½–1 fresh green or red chile, seeded and finely chopped

½ red bell pepper, seeded and chopped

3 tbsp chopped fresh mint

3 tbsp chopped fresh cilantro

pinch of salt

pinch of sugar

This sweet fruity salsa is fresh and fragrant, a wonderful foil to spicy food from the barbecue.

Using a sharp knife, cut off the top and bottom of the pineapple. Place upright on a board, then slice off the skin, cutting downward. Cut the flesh into slices, halve the slices, and remove the cores, if wished. Dice the flesh. Reserve any juice that accumulates as you cut the pineapple.

Place the pineapple in a nonmetallic bowl and stir in the lime juice, garlic, scallion, chile, and red bell pepper.

Stir in the mint and cilantro. Add the salt and sugar and stir well to combine all the ingredients. Cover and chill until ready to serve.

cook's tip

A fresh pineapple is ripe if it has a sweet aroma. The flesh will still be fairly firm to the touch. Stiff, fresh-looking leaves are a sign of good condition.

variation

Replace the pineapple with 3 juicy oranges, peeled and divided into segments.

crab & avocado

soft tacos

serves 4

15 minutes

10 minutes

8 soft corn tortillas
1 avocado
lime or lemon juice, for tossing
4–6 tbsp sour cream
9–10 oz/250–280 g cooked crabmeat
½ lime
½ fresh green chile, such as jalapeño
    or serrano, seeded and chopped
    or thinly sliced

1 ripe tomato, seeded and diced
½ small onion, finely chopped
2 tbsp chopped fresh cilantro
salsa of your choice, to serve
    (optional)

Crabmeat and avocado make an elegant yet very authentic filling for tacos. Eat one and you will be transported to a beach somewhere south of Acapulco!

variation

To transform into tostadas, fry the tortillas in a small amount of oil in a nonstick skillet until crisp. Top one crisp tortilla with the filling. Prepare a second tortilla with the filling and place on top of the first filled tortilla. Repeat once more, to make a small tower, top with shredded lettuce, and serve.

Heat the tortillas in an unoiled nonstick skillet, sprinkling them with a few drops of water as they heat; wrap in foil or a clean dish towel as you work to keep them warm.

Cut the avocado in half around the pit. Twist apart, then remove the pit with a knife. Carefully peel off the skin from the avocado, slice the flesh, and toss in lime juice to prevent discoloration.

Spread one tortilla with sour cream. Top with crabmeat, a squeeze of lime, and a sprinkling of chile, tomato, onion, cilantro, and avocado, adding a generous spoonful of salsa, if desired. Fold in the sides to form a cornet, repeat with the remaining tortillas, and serve at once.

fish tacos ensenada-style

serves 4

15 minutes

25 minutes

about 1 lb/450 g firm-fleshed white fish, such as red snapper or cod
1/4 tsp dried oregano
1/4 tsp ground cumin
1 tsp mild chili powder
2 garlic cloves, finely chopped
salt and pepper
3 tbsp all-purpose flour
vegetable oil, for frying

1/4 red cabbage, thinly sliced or shredded
juice of 2 limes
hot pepper sauce or salsa, to taste
8 corn tortillas
1 tbsp chopped fresh cilantro
1/2 onion, chopped (optional)
salsa of your choice

These tacos of fried fish chunks and red cabbage salad are served up in the cantinas and fondas of the coastal town of Ensenada, in Mexico's Baja California.

Place the fish on a plate and sprinkle with half the oregano, cumin, chili powder, and garlic, and salt and pepper to taste. Dust with the flour.

Heat the oil in a skillet until it is smoking, then fry the fish in several batches until it is golden on the outside and just tender in the middle. Remove from the skillet and place on paper towels to drain.

In a nonmetallic bowl, combine the cabbage with the remaining oregano, cumin, chili powder, and garlic, then stir in the lime juice and salt and hot pepper sauce to taste. Set aside.

Heat the tortillas in an unoiled nonstick skillet, sprinkling with a few drops of water as they heat; wrap the tortillas in foil or a clean dish towel as you work to keep them warm. Alternatively, heat through in a stack in the skillet, alternating the tortillas from the top to the bottom so that they warm evenly.

Place some of the warm fried fish in each tortilla with a large spoonful of the hot cabbage salad. Sprinkle with cilantro and onion, if using. Add some salsa and serve immediately.

fish & refried bean tostadas with green salsa

serves 4

15 minutes,
plus 30 minutes cooling

15 minutes

about 1 lb/450 g firm-fleshed white fish, such as red snapper or cod
½ cup fish stock or water mixed with 1 fish bouillon cube
¼ tsp ground cumin
¼ tsp mild chili powder
pinch of dried oregano
4 garlic cloves, finely chopped
salt and pepper
juice of ½ lemon or lime
8 soft corn tortillas
vegetable oil, for frying

14 oz/400 g canned refried beans, warmed with 2 tbsp water to thin
salsa of your choice
2–3 romaine lettuce leaves, shredded
3 tbsp chopped fresh cilantro
2 tbsp chopped onion

to garnish
sour cream
chopped fresh herbs

Crisp tostadas are topped with spiced fish, refried beans, and crunchy lettuce—perfect for a well-balanced lunch.

Place the fish in a pan with the stock, cumin, chili powder, oregano, garlic, and salt and pepper to taste. Stir and gently bring to a boil, then immediately remove the pan from the heat. Let the fish cool in the cooking liquid.

When cool enough to handle, remove from the fish from the liquid with a slotted spoon; reserve the cooking liquid. Break the fish up into bite-size pieces, place in a nonmetallic bowl, sprinkle with the lemon juice, and set aside until required.

To make the tostadas, fry the tortillas in a small amount of oil in a nonstick skillet until crisp. Spread the tostadas evenly with the warmed refried beans.

Gently reheat the fish with a little of the reserved cooking liquid in a pan, then spoon the fish on top of the beans. Top each tostada with some of the salsa, lettuce, cilantro, and onion. Garnish each one with a generous spoonful of sour cream and a sprinkling of chopped fresh herbs. Serve the tostadas immediately.

fish burritos

serves 4–6

15 minutes,
plus 30 minutes cooling

15 minutes

about 1 lb/450 g firm-fleshed white
    fish, such as red snapper or cod
salt and pepper
¼ tsp ground cumin
pinch of dried oregano
4 garlic cloves, finely chopped
½ cup fish stock or water mixed
    with 1 fish bouillon cube

juice of ½ lemon or lime
8 flour tortillas
2–3 romaine lettuce leaves, shredded
2 ripe tomatoes, diced
1 quantity Salsa Cruda (see page 97)
lemon slices, to serve

*You can use any seafood
you like in this tasty Mexican
snack. Tacos are eaten in the
hand, like sandwiches.*

variation

*Cook several peeled waxy
potatoes in the fish stock, then
dice and serve wrapped up
in the warm tortillas along with
the lettuce, fish, tomato, and
salsa. Or add sliced lime-dressed
avocado with the filling.*

Season the fish to taste with salt and pepper, then place in a pan with the cumin, oregano, garlic, and enough stock to cover.

Bring to a boil, then cook for 1 minute. Remove the pan from the heat. Let the fish cool in the cooking liquid for 30 minutes.

Remove the fish from the liquid with a slotted spoon and break up into bite-size pieces. Place in a nonmetallic bowl, sprinkle with the lemon juice, and set aside.

Heat the tortillas in an unoiled nonstick skillet, sprinkling them with a few drops of water as they heat; wrap the tortillas in foil or a clean dish towel as you work to keep them warm.

Arrange shredded lettuce in the center of one tortilla, spoon on a few big chunks of the fish, then sprinkle with the tomatoes. Add some of the Salsa Cruda. Repeat with the other tortillas and serve at once with lemon slices.

chicken tacos

from puebla

serves 4

10 minutes

15 minutes

8 soft corn tortillas

2 tsp vegetable oil

8–12 oz/225–350 g leftover cooked chicken, diced or shredded

salt and pepper

8 oz/225 g canned refried beans, warmed with 2 tbsp water to thin

1/4 tsp ground cumin

1/4 tsp dried oregano

1 avocado, pitted, peeled, sliced, and tossed with lime juice

Salsa Verde (see page 103) or salsa of your choice

1 canned chipotle chile in adobo marinade, chopped, or bottled chipotle salsa

3/4 cup sour cream

1/2 onion, chopped

handful of lettuce leaves

5 radishes, diced

Seasoned chicken fills these soft tacos, along with creamy refried beans, avocado, smoky chipotle, and sour cream. A feast of tastes!

variation

Replace the chicken with 1 lb/450 g ground beef, browned with a seasoning of chopped onion, mild chili powder, and ground cumin to taste.

Heat the tortillas through in an unoiled nonstick skillet in a stack, alternating the tortillas from the top to the bottom so that they warm evenly. Wrap in foil or a clean dish towel to keep them warm.

Heat the oil in a skillet. Add the chicken and heat through. Season to taste with salt and pepper.

Combine the warmed refried beans with the cumin and oregano.

Spread one tortilla with the refried beans, then top with a spoonful of the chicken, a slice or two of avocado, a little salsa, chipotle to taste, a spoonful of sour cream, and a sprinkling of onion, lettuce, and radishes. Season to taste with salt and pepper, then roll up as tightly as you can. Repeat with the remaining tortillas and serve at once.

chile verde tacos
with pinto beans

serves 4

10 minutes

10–15 minutes

8 soft corn tortillas
vegetable oil, for oiling
14 oz/400 g canned pinto beans
⅓ quantity Chile Verde
   (see page 205)
3 ripe tomatoes, diced
½ onion, chopped
2 tbsp finely chopped fresh cilantro

to garnish
sour cream
mild chili powder

to serve
salsa of your choice
shredded lettuce

This is also an ideal way of using up any leftover spicy stewed meat—use in place of the Chile Verde and you have an almost instant meal!

variation

For a tostada version, heat tostadas (crisp tortillas) under the broiler, then spread with warmed, slightly thinned canned refried beans and top with the Chile Verde, shredded lettuce, a little grated romano cheese, salsa, onion, fresh cilantro, and sour cream.

Heat the tortillas in a lightly oiled nonstick skillet; wrap in foil or a clean dish towel as you work to keep them warm.

Drain the beans, reserving a few tablespoons of the liquid. Heat the beans in a pan with the reserved liquid.

Heat through the Chile Verde in a pan until just boiling.

Spoon some of the drained beans on to a warmed tortilla. Top with the warmed Chile Verde, then sprinkle with tomatoes, onion, and cilantro. Roll up and repeat with the remaining tortillas. Garnish with a spoonful of sour cream and a sprinkling of chili powder, then serve at once with salsa and shredded lettuce.

chicken tostadas with green salsa & chipotle

serves 4–6

20 minutes

15 minutes

6 soft corn tortillas

vegetable oil, for frying

1 lb/450 g skinned, boned chicken breast or thigh, cut into strips or small pieces

1 cup chicken stock

2 garlic cloves, finely chopped

14 oz/400 g Refried Beans (see page 145) or canned

large pinch of ground cumin

2 cups grated cheese

1 tbsp chopped fresh cilantro

2 ripe tomatoes, diced

handful of crisp lettuce leaves, such as romaine or iceberg, shredded

4–6 radishes, diced

3 scallions, thinly sliced

1 ripe avocado, pitted, peeled, diced or sliced, and tossed with lime juice

sour cream, to taste

1–2 canned chipotle chiles in adobo marinade or dried chipotle, reconstituted (see page 100) and cut into thin strips

Chicken makes a delicate yet satisfying topping for crisp tostadas. You do not need to prepare chicken especially for this recipe—any leftover chicken is equally delicious.

To make the tostadas, fry the tortillas in a small amount of oil in a nonstick skillet until crisp. Set aside.

Place the chicken in a pan with the stock and garlic. Bring to a boil, then reduce the heat and cook for 1–2 minutes, or until the chicken begins to turn opaque.

Remove the chicken from the heat and let stand in its hot liquid to cook through.

Heat the beans in a separate pan with enough water to form a smooth purée. Add the cumin and keep warm.

Reheat the tostadas under a preheated medium broiler, if necessary. Spread the hot beans on the tostadas, then sprinkle with the cheese. Lift the cooked chicken from the liquid and divide between the tostadas. Top with the cilantro, tomatoes, lettuce, radishes, scallions, avocado, sour cream, and a few strips of chipotle. Serve immediately.

vegetable tostadas

serves 4

10 minutes

20 minutes

4 soft corn tortillas

2–3 tbsp virgin olive oil or vegetable oil, plus extra for frying

2 potatoes, diced

1 carrot, diced

3 garlic cloves, finely chopped

1 red bell pepper, seeded and diced

1 tsp mild chili powder

1 tsp paprika

½ tsp ground cumin

3–4 ripe tomatoes, diced

4 oz/115 g green beans, blanched and cut into bite-size lengths

several large pinches of dried oregano

14 oz/400 g cooked black beans, drained

2 cups crumbled feta cheese

3–4 romaine lettuce leaves, shredded

3–4 scallions, thinly sliced

Top a crisp tostada with spicy vegetables and you have a fabulous vegetarian feast!

To make the tostadas, fry the tortillas in a small amount of oil in a nonstick skillet until crisp. Set aside.

Heat the remaining oil in the skillet. Add the potatoes and carrot and cook for 10 minutes, or until softened. Add the garlic, red bell pepper, chili powder, paprika, and cumin. Cook for 2–3 minutes, or until the bell peppers have softened.

Add the tomatoes, green beans, and oregano. Cook for 8–10 minutes, or until the vegetables are tender and form a sauce-like mixture. The mixture should not be too dry; add a little water if necessary to keep it moist.

Preheat the broiler to medium. Heat the black beans in a pan with a tiny amount of water and keep warm. Reheat the tostadas under the hot broiler.

Layer the beans over the hot tostadas, then sprinkle with the cheese and top with a few spoonfuls of the hot vegetables in sauce. Sprinkle each tostada with the lettuce and scallions and serve at once.

broccoli enchiladas
in mild chili salsa

serves 4

15 minutes

40 minutes

1 lb/450 g broccoli florets
1 cup ricotta cheese
1 garlic clove, chopped
1/2 tsp ground cumin
6–8 oz/175–200 g Cheddar cheese, grated
6–8 tbsp freshly grated Parmesan cheese
1 egg, lightly beaten
salt and pepper
4–6 flour tortillas

vegetable oil, for oiling
1 quantity Mild Red Chili Sauce (see page 86)
1 cup chicken or vegetable stock
1/2 onion, finely chopped
3–4 tbsp chopped fresh cilantro
3 ripe tomatoes, diced
hot salsa, to serve

This is reminiscent of a sort of Mexican spiced cannelloni, with flour tortillas taking the place of the pasta tubes.

Preheat the oven to 375°F/190°C. Bring a pan of salted water to a boil, add the broccoli, return to a boil, and blanch for 1 minute. Drain, refresh under cold running water, then drain again. Cut off the stalks, peel, and chop. Dice the heads.

Mix the broccoli with the ricotta cheese, garlic, cumin, and half the Cheddar and Parmesan cheeses in a bowl. Mix in the egg and season to taste with salt and pepper.

Heat the tortillas in a lightly oiled nonstick skillet; wrap in foil or a clean dish towel as you work to keep them warm. Fill the tortillas with the broccoli mixture, rolling them up.

Arrange the tortilla rolls in an ovenproof dish, then pour the chili sauce over the top. Pour over the stock.

Top with the remaining Cheddar and Parmesan cheeses and bake in the oven for 30 minutes. Sprinkle with the onion, chopped cilantro, and tomatoes and serve with a hot salsa.

cheese enchiladas
with mole flavors

serves 4–6

15 minutes

25–30 minutes

8 soft corn tortillas

vegetable oil, for oiling

2 cups Mole Poblano (see page 91) or bottled mole paste

about 2 cups grated cheese, such as Cheddar, mozzarella, Asiago, or Mexican queso oaxaco—one type or a combination

1 cup chicken or vegetable stock

5 scallions, thinly sliced

2–3 tbsp chopped fresh cilantro

handful of romaine lettuce leaves, shredded

1 avocado, pitted, peeled, diced, and tossed in lime juice

4 tbsp sour cream

salsa of your choice

Mole sauce makes a delicious enchilada—a good reason to make yourself a big pot of Mole Poblano (see page 91). But if you are short of time, you can always use bottled mole paste instead.

Preheat the oven to 375°F/190°C. Heat the tortillas in a lightly oiled nonstick skillet; wrap in foil or a clean dish towel as you work to keep them warm.

Dip the tortillas into the mole sauce and pile up on a plate. Fill the inside of the top sauced tortilla with a few spoonfuls of grated cheese. Roll up and arrange in a shallow ovenproof dish. Repeat with the remaining tortillas, reserving a handful of the cheese to sprinkle over the top.

Pour the rest of the mole sauce over the rolled tortillas, then pour the stock over the top. Sprinkle with the reserved cheese and cover with foil.

Bake in the preheated oven for 20 minutes, or until the tortillas are piping hot and the cheese filling melts.

Arrange the scallions, cilantro, lettuce, avocado, and sour cream on top. Add salsa to taste. Serve at once.

santa fe red chili

enchiladas

serves 4

15 minutes

35 minutes

2–3 tbsp masa harina or 1 corn tortilla, crushed or crumbled

4 tbsp mild chili powder, such as New Mexico

2 tbsp paprika

2 garlic cloves, finely chopped

1/4 tsp ground cumin

pinch of ground cinnamon

pinch of ground allspice

pinch of dried oregano

4 cups vegetable, chicken, or beef stock, simmering

1 tbsp lime juice

8 flour tortillas

about 1 lb/450 g cooked chicken or pork, cut into pieces

3/4 cup grated cheese

1 tbsp virgin olive oil

4 eggs

to serve

1/2 onion, finely chopped

1 tbsp finely chopped fresh cilantro

salsa of your choice

These enchiladas are served stacked, in the traditional New Mexican style, but you can always roll them up with the filling, if you prefer.

Preheat the oven to 350°F/180°C. In a bowl, mix the masa harina with the chili powder, paprika, garlic, cumin, cinnamon, allspice, oregano, and enough water to form a thin paste. Transfer to a food processor or blender and process until smooth.

Stir the paste into the simmering stock, reduce the heat, and cook until it thickens slightly. Remove the sauce from the heat and stir in the lime juice.

Dip the tortillas into the warm sauce. Cover one tortilla with some of the cooked meat. Top with a second dipped tortilla and more meat filling. Make 3 more towers in this way, then transfer to an ovenproof dish.

Pour the remaining sauce over the tortillas, then sprinkle with the grated cheese. Bake in the oven for 15–20 minutes, or until the cheese melts.

Meanwhile, heat the oil in a nonstick skillet and cook the eggs until the whites are set and the yolks are still soft.

To serve the enchiladas, top each with a fried egg. Serve with the onion mixed with cilantro and a salsa.

chicken tortilla flutes
with guacamole

serves 4

15 minutes

15 minutes

8 soft corn tortillas
12 oz/350 g cooked chicken, diced
1 tsp mild chili powder
1 onion, chopped
2 tbsp finely chopped fresh cilantro
salt
1–2 tbsp sour cream
vegetable oil, for frying

to serve

1 quantity Guacamole
(see page 29)
salsa of your choice

These crisply fried, rolled tortillas are known as flauta, meaning "flutes", because of their delicate, long shape.

Heat the tortillas in an unoiled nonstick skillet in a stack, moving the tortillas from the top to the bottom so that they warm evenly. Wrap in foil or a clean dish towel to keep them warm.

Place the chicken in a large bowl with the chili powder, half the chopped onion and cilantro, and salt to taste. Add enough sour cream to bind the mixture together.

Arrange 2 corn tortillas on the counter so that they are overlapping, then spoon some of the filling down the center. Roll up very tightly and secure in place with a toothpick or two. Repeat with the remaining tortillas and filling.

Heat enough oil for frying in a deep skillet until hot and fry the rolls until golden and crisp. Carefully remove the rolls from the oil and drain on paper towels.

Serve with the Guacamole, salsa, and the remaining onion and cilantro.

variation

Replace the chicken with seafood, such as cooked, shelled shrimp or crabmeat, and serve the rolls with lemon wedges.

pork quesadillas with pinto beans

serves 4

15 minutes

15–20 minutes

1 quantity Carnitas (see page 209) or about 3½ oz/100 g cooked pork strips per person

1 ripe tomato, seeded and diced

½ onion, chopped

3 tbsp chopped fresh cilantro

4 large flour tortillas

12 oz/350 g grated or thinly sliced cheese, such as mozzarella or Swiss

about 2 cups cooked drained pinto beans

hot salsa of your choice or bottled hot sauce, to taste

pickled jalapeño chiles, cut into thin rings, to taste

vegetable oil, for frying

to serve

pickled chiles

mixed salad

These melt-in-the-mouth tortilla pockets have a lovely pork, bean, and melted cheese filling. Any leftover cooked meat may be used instead of the Carnitas.

Heat the Carnitas in a pan and keep hot over low heat.

Combine the tomato, onion, and cilantro in a bowl and set aside.

Heat a tortilla in an unoiled nonstick skillet. Sprinkle the tortilla with cheese, then top with some of the meat, beans, and reserved tomato mixture. Add salsa and chile rings to taste. Fold over the sides of the tortilla to make a pocket.

Heat the pockets gently on each side in the skillet, adding a few drops of oil to keep it all supple and succulent, until the tortilla is golden and the cheese inside has melted. Keep warm. Repeat with the remaining tortillas and filling.

Transfer the quesadillas to a plate and serve at once with pickled chiles and salad.

casserole of tortilla chips & chorizo

serves 6–8

10 minutes

1 hour 15 minutes

12 stale tortillas, cut into strips
1 tbsp vegetable oil
2–3 fresh chorizo sausages, thinly sliced or diced
2 garlic cloves, finely chopped
8 oz/225 g chopped canned tomatoes
3 tbsp chopped fresh cilantro

salt and pepper
2 cups chicken or vegetable stock
2 cups grated cheese
1 onion, finely chopped, to garnish
salsa of your choice, to serve (optional)

Called chilaquiles in Mexico, this dish turns everyday leftovers into something quite special! Excellent served for brunch with a fried egg.

Preheat the oven to 375°F/190°C. Place the tortilla strips in a roasting pan, toss with the oil, and bake in the oven for 30 minutes, or until they are crisp and golden.

Brown the chorizo with the garlic in a skillet until the meat is cooked through; pour away any excess fat. Add the tomatoes and cilantro and season to taste with salt and pepper. Set aside.

In an ovenproof dish about 12 inches/30 cm square, layer the tortilla strips and chorizo mixture, finishing with the tortilla strips.

Pour the stock over the top of the dish, then sprinkle with the cheese. Bake in the oven at the same temperature for 40 minutes, or until the tortilla chips are fairly soft.

Sprinkle with chopped onion and serve immediately with salsa, if wished.

green chile & chicken chilaquiles

serves 4–6

20 minutes

1 hour

12 stale tortillas, cut into strips

1 tbsp vegetable oil

1 small cooked chicken, meat removed from the bones and cut into bite-size pieces

Salsa Verde (see page 103)

3 tbsp chopped fresh cilantro

1 tsp finely chopped fresh oregano or thyme

4 garlic cloves, finely chopped

¼ tsp ground cumin

3 cups grated cheese, such as Cheddar, manchego, or mozzarella

2 cups chicken stock

about 1 cup freshly grated Parmesan cheese

to serve

1½ cups sour cream

3–5 scallions, thinly sliced

pickled chiles

Easy to put together, this dish makes a perfect mid-week supper. Use tortilla chips instead of baking the tortillas, if you prefer.

variation

For a vegetarian Mexicana filling, add diced sautéed tofu (bean curd) and corn in place of the cooked chicken.

Preheat the oven to 375°F/190°C. Place the tortilla strips in a roasting pan, toss with the oil, and bake in the oven for 30 minutes, or until they are crisp and golden.

Arrange the chicken in a 9- x 13-inch/23- x 33-cm flameproof casserole, then sprinkle with half the salsa, cilantro, oregano, garlic, cumin, and some of the Cheddar, manchego, or mozzarella cheese. Repeat these layers and top with the tortilla strips.

Pour the stock over the top, then sprinkle with the remaining cheese.

Bake in the oven at the same temperature for 30 minutes, or until heated through and the cheese is lightly golden in areas.

Serve with a spoonful of sour cream, sliced scallions, and pickled chiles to taste.

tamales

serves 4–6

30 minutes,
plus 3 hours soaking

40–60 minutes

8–10 corn husks or several banana
leaves, cut into 12-inch/30-cm
squares

6 tbsp shortening

1/2 tsp salt

pinch of sugar

pinch of ground cumin

8 oz/225 g masa harina

1/2 tsp baking powder

about 1 cup beef, chicken, or
vegetable stock

filling

1 cup cooked corn kernels, mixed
with a little grated cheese and
chopped fresh green chile, or pork
simmered in a mild chili sauce

to serve

shredded lettuce

tomato wedges

salsa of your choice

*Traditional Mexican fare, tamales
are large dumplings of corn flour,
stuffed with a moist filling, then
wrapped in either banana leaves
or husks of corn. They make
attractive party food.*

If using corn husks, soak in enough hot water to cover for at least 3 hours
or overnight. If using banana leaves, warm them by placing over an open
flame for just a few seconds, to make them pliable.

To make the tamale dough, beat the shortening until fluffy in a bowl, then
beat in the salt, sugar, cumin, masa harina, and baking powder until the
mixture resembles very fine crumbs.

Add the stock very gradually, in several batches, beating until the mixture
becomes fluffy and resembles whipped cream.

Spread 1–2 tablespoons of the tamale mixture on either a soaked and
drained corn husk or a piece of pliable heated banana leaf.

Spoon in the filling. Fold the sides of the husks or leaves over the filling to
enclose. Wrap each pocket in a square of foil and arrange in a steamer.

Pour enough hot water into the bottom of the steamer, cover, and boil.
Steam for 40–60 minutes, topping up the water in the bottom of the
steamer when needed. Remove the tamales and serve with shredded
lettuce, tomato wedges, and salsa.

burritos of lamb &
black beans

serves 4

15 minutes,
plus 4 hours marinating

15–20 minutes

1 lb 7 oz/650 g lean lamb
3 garlic cloves, finely chopped
juice of 1/2 lime
1/2 tsp mild chili powder
1/2 tsp ground cumin
large pinch of dried oregano leaves, crushed
1–2 tbsp extra-virgin olive oil
salt and pepper

2 1/2 cups cooked black beans, seasoned with a little cumin, salt, and pepper
4 large flour tortillas
2–3 tbsp chopped fresh cilantro, plus a few sprigs to garnish
salsa, preferably Chipotle Salsa (see page 99)
lime wedges, to serve (optional)

Stir-fried marinated lamb strips are paired with earthy black beans in these tasty burritos.

Slice the lamb into thin strips, then combine with the garlic, lime juice, chili powder, cumin, oregano, and oil in a nonmetallic bowl. Season to taste with salt and pepper. Cover and let marinate in the refrigerator for 4 hours.

Warm the black beans with a little water in a pan.

Heat the tortillas in an unoiled nonstick skillet, sprinkling them with a few drops of water as they heat; wrap the tortillas in foil or a clean dish towel as you work to keep them warm. Alternatively, heat through in a stack in the skillet, moving the tortillas from the top to the bottom so that they warm evenly. Wrap to keep warm.

Stir-fry the lamb in a heavy-bottomed nonstick skillet over high heat until browned on all sides. Remove the skillet from the heat.

variation

Add a spoonful or two of cooked rice to each burrito.

Spoon some of the beans and browned meat into a tortilla, sprinkle with cilantro, then add a little salsa and fold in the sides. Repeat with the remaining tortillas. Garnish with cilantro sprigs and serve at once with lime wedges and any spare salsa, if wished.

mexican beans

serves 4–6

15 minutes,
plus 8 hours soaking

2 hours 30 minutes

3 cups dried pinto or pink beans
1 fresh mint sprig
1 fresh thyme sprig
1 fresh flatleaf parsley sprig
1 onion, cut into chunks
salt

shredded scallion, to garnish
warmed flour or soft corn tortillas,
  to serve

A pot of beans, bubbling away on the stove, is the basic everyday food of Mexico—delicious and healthy!

cook's tip

If using the beans for Refried Beans (see page 145), do not drain as the liquid is required for the recipe.

The length of time the beans take to cook will depend on the age of the beans—old beans take longer than younger beans; the mineral content of the water matters, too.

Pick through the beans and remove any bits of grit or stone. Cover the beans with cold water and let soak overnight. If you want to cut down on soaking time, bring the beans to a boil in a pan, cook for 5 minutes, then remove from the heat and let stand, covered, for 2 hours.

Drain the beans, place in a pan, and cover with fresh water. Add the herb sprigs. Bring to a boil, then reduce the heat to very low and cook gently, covered, for 2 hours, or until the beans are tender. The best way to check that they are done is to sample a bean or two every so often after 1¾ hours' cooking time.

Add the onion chunks and continue to cook until the onion and beans are very tender.

To serve as a side dish, drain, season to taste with salt, and serve in a bowl lined with warmed tortillas, garnished with shredded scallion. Alternatively, see Cook's Tip.

refried beans

serves 4–6

15 minutes

40 minutes

1 quantity Mexican Beans, with their cooking liquid (see page 142)

½ cup vegetable oil or shortening

1–2 onions, chopped

½ tsp ground cumin

salt

2¼ cups grated Cheddar cheese (optional)

One of Mexico's most famous dishes, refried beans, or frijoles refritos, *is incredibly versatile. Serve them piled on to crisp tostadas or crusty rolls, spooned beside rice, or rolled into a tortilla.*

variation

Add several browned, broken-up chorizo sausages to the beans, along with a small can of sardines, mashed to a paste. Serve stuffed into crusty rolls for a classic mollete, *or as a party dip. Good spread on to crisp tostadas for an afternoon pick-me-up.*

Place two-thirds of the cooked beans, with their cooking liquid, in a food processor or blender and process to a purée. Stir in the remaining whole beans. Set aside.

Heat the oil in a heavy-bottomed skillet. Add the onions and cook until they are very soft. Sprinkle with cumin and salt to taste.

Ladle in a cupful of the bean mixture, and cook, stirring constantly, until the beans reduce down to a thick mixture; the beans will darken slightly as they cook.

Continue adding the bean mixture, a ladleful at a time, stirring and allowing the liquid to reduce down before adding the next ladleful. You should end up with a thick, chunky purée.

If using cheese, sprinkle it over the beans and cover tightly until the heat in the skillet melts the cheese. Alternatively, place under a preheated medium broiler to melt the cheese. Serve immediately.

mexican **refried beans**
"with everything"

serves 4

15 minutes

25 minutes

1–2 tbsp vegetable oil

1–1 ½ large onions, chopped

4½ oz/125 g bacon strips, cut into small pieces

3–4 garlic cloves, finely chopped

about 1 tsp ground cumin

½ tsp mild chili powder

14 oz/400 g canned tomatoes, diced and drained, reserving about ⅔–¾ cup of their juice

14 oz/400 g canned refried beans, broken up into pieces

generous ⅓ cup beer

14 oz/400 g canned pinto beans, drained

salt and pepper

to serve

warmed flour tortillas

sour cream

sliced pickled chiles

These are refried beans fit for a fiesta, rich with everything—bacon, fried onions, tomatoes, even a little beer! As delicious as it sounds!

variation

Top the dish with grated cheese, then pop under a preheated broiler to melt and sizzle. Serve at once. This makes a luscious filling for warmed flour tortillas.

Heat the oil in a skillet. Add the onion and bacon and cook for 5 minutes, or until they are just turning brown. Stir in the garlic, cumin, and chili powder and continue to cook for 1 minute. Add the tomatoes and cook over medium–high heat until the liquid has evaporated.

Add the refried beans and mash lightly in the skillet with the tomato mixture, adding beer as needed to thin out the beans and make them smoother. Reduce the heat and cook, stirring, until the mixture is smooth and creamy.

Add the pinto beans and stir well to combine; if the mixture is too thick, add a little of the reserved tomato juice. Adjust the spicing to taste. Season to taste with salt and pepper and serve with warmed tortillas, sour cream, and pickled chiles.

spicy fragrant
black bean chili

serves 4

15 minutes,
plus 8 hours soaking

2 hours 45 minutes

2¼ cups dried black beans
2 tbsp olive oil
1 onion, chopped
5 garlic cloves, coarsely chopped
2 bacon strips, diced (optional)
½–1 tsp ground cumin
½–1 tsp mild red chili powder

1 red bell pepper, diced
1 carrot, diced
14 oz/400 g fresh tomatoes, diced,
   or canned, chopped
1 bunch fresh cilantro, coarsely
   chopped
salt and pepper

*Black beans are fragrant
and flavorful; enjoy this
chilied bean stew Mexican style
with soft tortillas, or Californian
style in a bowl with crisp
tortilla chips crumbled in.*

cook's tip

*You can use canned beans,
if wished: drain and use
1 cup water in place of the
reserved bean cooking liquid.*

Soak the beans overnight, then drain. Place in a pan, cover with water, and bring to a boil. Boil for 10 minutes, then reduce the heat and simmer for 1½ hours, or until tender. Drain well, reserving 1 cup of the cooking liquid.

Heat the oil in a skillet. Add the onion and garlic and cook for 2 minutes, stirring. Add the bacon, if using, and cook, stirring occasionally, until the bacon is cooked and the onion is softened.

Stir in the cumin and chili powder and continue to cook for a moment or two. Add the red bell pepper, carrot, and tomatoes. Cook over medium heat for 5 minutes.

Add half the cilantro and the beans and their reserved liquid. Season to taste with salt and pepper. Simmer for 30–45 minutes, or until very flavorful and thickened.

Stir in the remaining cilantro, adjust the seasoning, and serve at once.

rice with lime

serves 4

5 minutes

15 minutes

2 tbsp vegetable oil
1 small onion, finely chopped
3 garlic cloves, finely chopped
scant 1 cup long-grain rice
2 cups chicken or vegetable stock

juice of 1 lime
1 tbsp chopped fresh cilantro
sautéed plantain (see Cook's Tip),
   to garnish (optional)
lime wedges, to serve (optional)

The tangy citrus taste of lime is marvelous with all sorts of rice dishes. Although not typically Mexican, you could add wild rice to this dish, if liked.

Heat the oil in a flameproof casserole or heavy-bottomed pan. Add the onion and garlic and cook gently, stirring occasionally, for 2 minutes. Add the rice and cook for an additional minute, stirring. Pour in the stock, increase the heat, and bring the rice to a boil. Reduce the heat to a very low simmer.

Cover and cook the rice for 10 minutes, or until the rice is just tender and the liquid is absorbed.

Sprinkle in the lime juice and fork the rice to fluff up and to mix in the juice. Sprinkle with the cilantro, then garnish with sautéed plantain and serve with lime wedges, if wished.

cook's tip

Garnish the rice with sautéed plantain: slice a ripe peeled plantain, preferably on the diagonal, then fry in a heavy-bottomed skillet in a small amount of oil until browned in places and tender. Arrange in the bowl of rice.

variation

Fork about 2 cups cooked corn kernels into the rice when it is almost but not quite cooked, then allow the corn to warm through as the rice finishes cooking. Sprinkle with diced cucumber and a squeeze of lime juice to add a fresh tang.

cumin rice with
bell peppers

serves 4

20 minutes

20 minutes

2 tbsp butter

1 tbsp vegetable oil

1 green bell pepper, seeded and sliced

1 red bell pepper, seeded and sliced

3 scallions, thinly sliced

3–4 garlic cloves, finely chopped

scant 1 cup long-grain rice

1 1/2 tsp cumin seeds

1/2 tsp dried oregano or marjoram, crushed

2 cups chicken or vegetable stock

Cumin seeds add a distinctive flavor to this colorful rice dish. Serve as a side dish with any roasted or grilled meat.

variation

Fold through a portion or two of black beans, and serve as a side dish with roasted meat or poultry.

Heat the butter and oil in a flameproof casserole or heavy-bottomed pan. Add the bell peppers and cook until softened.

Add the scallions, garlic, rice, and cumin seeds. Cook for 5 minutes, or until the rice turns slightly golden.

Add the oregano and stock to the casserole, bring to a boil, then reduce the heat and cook for 5 minutes.

Cover with a clean dish towel and remove the casserole from the heat. Let steam for 10 minutes, depending upon the age and maturity of the rice. If the rice is mature, extend the initial cooking time to 10 minutes.

Fluff up the rice with a fork and serve at once.

green rice

 serves 4

 20 minutes

 25 minutes

1–2 onions, halved and unpeeled

6–8 large garlic cloves, unpeeled

1 large mild fresh chile or 1 green bell pepper and 1 small fresh green chile

1 bunch fresh cilantro leaves, chopped

1 cup chicken or vegetable stock

⅓ cup vegetable or olive oil

scant 1 cup long-grain rice

salt and pepper

fresh cilantro sprig, to garnish

A paste of roasted onions, garlic, and chiles, puréed with lots of green cilantro leaves, gives this rice a lovely fresh color and stunning taste.

cook's tip

Leftover green rice is delicious mixed with beef and/or ground pork for savory meatballs, or as a filling for bell peppers.

Heat an unoiled heavy-bottomed skillet and cook the onion, garlic, chile, and bell pepper, if using, until lightly charred on all sides, including the cut sides of the onions. Cover and let cool.

When cool enough to handle, remove the skin and seeds from the chile and bell pepper, if using. Chop the flesh.

Remove the skins from the cooled onion and garlic and finely chop.

Place the vegetables in a food processor or blender with the chopped cilantro leaves and stock, then process to a smooth thin purée.

Heat the oil in a heavy-bottomed pan. Add the rice and cook until it is glistening and lightly browned in places, stirring to prevent it burning. Add the vegetable purée, cover, and cook over medium–low heat for 10–15 minutes, or until the rice is just tender.

Fluff up the rice with a fork, then cover and let stand for 5 minutes. Adjust the seasoning, garnish with a cilantro sprig, and serve.

rice with black beans

serves 4

15 minutes

15 minutes

1 onion, chopped

5 garlic cloves, chopped

1 cup chicken or vegetable stock

2 tbsp vegetable oil

scant 1 cup long-grain rice

1 cup liquid from cooking black beans, plus a few beans

1/2 tsp ground cumin

salt and pepper

to garnish

3–5 scallions, thinly sliced

2 tbsp chopped fresh cilantro

Any kind of bean cooking liquid is delicious for cooking rice—black beans are particularly good for their startling pinkish-gray color and earthy flavor.

variation

Instead of black beans, use pinto beans or chickpeas. Proceed as above and serve with any savory spicy sauce, or as an accompaniment to roasted meat.

Place the onion in a food processor or blender with the garlic and stock and process until the consistency of a chunky sauce.

Heat the oil in a heavy-bottomed skillet and cook the rice until it is golden. Add the onion mixture with the cooking liquid from the black beans and any beans. Add the cumin and salt and pepper to taste.

Cover the skillet and cook over medium–low heat for 10 minutes, or until the rice is just tender. The rice should be a pinkish-gray color and taste delicious.

Fluff up the rice with a fork, then cover and let stand for 5 minutes. Serve sprinkled with thinly sliced scallions and chopped cilantro.

lentils simmered with fruits

serves 4

5 minutes

45 minutes

²/₃ cup brown or green lentils

about 4 cups water

2 tbsp vegetable oil

3 small to medium onions, chopped

4 garlic cloves, coarsely chopped

1 large cooking apple, coarsely chopped

about ¼ ripe pineapple, peeled and coarsely chopped

2 tomatoes, seeded and diced

1 almost ripe banana, cut into bite-size pieces

salt

cayenne pepper, to taste

fresh parsley sprig, to garnish

Although this might seem an unusual combination, when you serve up this traditional dish you'll see how the fruits lighten the earthy lentils to create a delicious side dish.

variation

Instead of lentils, prepare the dish using cooked pinto or pink beans.

Combine the lentils with the water in a pan, then bring to a boil. Reduce the heat and simmer over low heat for 40 minutes, or until the lentils are tender. Do not let them become mushy.

Meanwhile, heat the oil in a skillet and cook the onions and garlic until lightly browned and softened. Add the apple and continue to cook until golden. Add the pineapple, heat through, stirring, then add the tomatoes. Cook over medium heat until thickened, stirring occasionally

Drain the lentils, reserving ½ cup of the cooking liquid. Add the drained lentils to the sauce, stirring in the reserved liquid if necessary. Heat through for a minute to let the flavors mingle.

Add the banana to the skillet, then season to taste with salt and cayenne pepper. Serve garnished with a parsley sprig.

dry soup of thin noodles

 serves 4

 15 minutes

 30–40 minutes

12 oz/350 g very thin dried pasta, such as fideo or capellini

2–3 bay leaves

2–3 fresh chorizo sausages, sliced

1 onion, chopped

1 green bell pepper or mild fresh green chile, such as Anaheim or poblano, seeded and chopped

4–5 garlic cloves, finely chopped

1 ½ cups strained tomatoes

1 ½ cups hot chicken, meat, or vegetable stock

¼ tsp ground cumin

½ tsp mild red chili powder

pinch of dried oregano

3 cups grated sharp Cheddar cheese

2 tbsp chopped fresh cilantro

This curiously named baked dish is made with pasta, tortillas, or rice, and has an appetizing dense texture. It often has a cheesy topping, and is served either as a first course, such as an Italian might, or as a comforting supper dish.

Cook the pasta in a large pan of boiling salted water with the bay leaves until only just tender. Drain and discard the bay leaves. Rinse the pasta to rid it of excess starch. Let drain.

Preheat the oven to 400°F/200°C. Heat an unoiled skillet, add the chorizo, and cook until it begins to brown. Add the onion, green bell pepper or chile, and garlic and cook, stirring occasionally, until all the vegetables are softened.

Add the strained tomatoes, stock, cumin, chili powder, and oregano and remove the skillet from the heat.

Toss the pasta with the hot sauce, then transfer to an ovenproof dish. Smooth the surface with a spoon, then cover with a generous layer of the grated cheese.

Bake in the oven for 15 minutes, or until the top is lightly browned and the pasta is heated through. Serve at once, sprinkled with chopped cilantro.

main courses

In Mexico, the main meal is traditionally served at midday, a gloriously relaxed affair, usually consisting of a fish or meat dish. Using a wonderful mix of flavors and cooking methods, a result of Mexico's complex and colorful past, the cuisine offers some delicious entrées.

Eggs are cooked with spices, tangy herbs, garlic, and tomatoes to make an appetizing topping to tortillas, while fish is given a lift with subtle aromatic marinades—salmon broiled with a smoky chili dressing or bass baked with lime and cilantro is a feast of Mexican flavors.

Sizzling strips of beef rolled up with crunchy vegetables in a tortilla is classic Mexican fare, as is pork stewed with mild chiles, sweet plantains, and potatoes—an inspiring marriage of flavors and textures. Or try the traditional Mexican way of simmering pork until meltingly tender, then frying it until crisp and golden. Cook chicken with Mexican flair by stewing it with vegetables and fruits, or marinate chicken wings in tequila, to tenderize them and add flavor before grilling.

Serve any of the dishes in this chapter to bring a touch of sunny Mexico to your meals, whether it is a family lunch or a dinner with friends.

jalisco-style eggs

serves 4

15 minutes

20 minutes

4 soft corn tortillas

1 avocado

lime or lemon juice, for tossing

6 oz/175 g fresh chorizo sausage, sliced or diced

2 tbsp butter or water, for cooking

4 eggs

4 tbsp crumbled feta cheese

salsa of your choice

1 tbsp chopped fresh cilantro

1 tbsp finely chopped scallions

This hearty breakfast dish from Jalisco is a classic Mexican way of serving eggs—a feast of flavors!

Heat the tortillas in an unoiled nonstick skillet, sprinkling them with a few drops of water as they heat; wrap the tortillas in foil or a clean dish towel as you work to keep them warm. Alternatively, heat through in a stack in the skillet, moving the tortillas from the top to the bottom so that they warm evenly. Wrap to keep them warm.

Cut the avocado in half around the pit. Twist apart, then remove the pit with a knife. Carefully peel off the skin, dice the flesh, and toss in lime juice to prevent discoloration.

Heat a separate skillet, add the chorizo, and cook until browned, then arrange on each warmed tortilla. Keep warm.

Meanwhile, heat the butter or water in the nonstick skillet, break in an egg, and cook until the white is set but the yolk is still soft. Remove from the skillet and place on top of one tortilla. Keep warm.

Cook the remaining eggs in the same way, adding to the tortillas.

Arrange the avocado, cheese, and a spoonful of salsa on each tortilla. Add the cilantro and scallions and serve.

migas

serves 4

10 minutes

12 minutes

2 tbsp butter

6 garlic cloves, finely chopped

1 fresh green chile, such as jalapeño or serrano, seeded and diced

1½ tsp ground cumin

6 ripe tomatoes, coarsely chopped

8 eggs, lightly beaten

8–10 soft corn tortillas, cut into strips and fried until crisp, or an equal amount of not too salty tortilla chips

4 tbsp chopped fresh cilantro

3–4 scallions, thinly sliced

mild chili powder, to garnish

A wonderful brunch or late-night supper dish, this is made by scrambling eggs with chiles, tomatoes, and crisp tortilla chips.

Melt half the butter in a pan. Add the garlic and chile and cook until softened but not browned. Add the cumin and cook for 30 seconds, stirring, then add the tomatoes and cook over medium heat for an additional 3–4 minutes, or until the tomato juices have evaporated. Remove from the pan and set aside.

Melt the remaining butter in a skillet over low heat and pour in the beaten eggs. Cook, stirring, until the eggs begin to set.

Add the reserved chile tomato mixture to the skillet, stirring gently to mix into the eggs.

Carefully add the tortilla strips or chips and continue cooking, stirring once or twice, until the eggs are the consistency you wish. The tortillas should be pliable and chewy.

Transfer to a serving plate and surround with the cilantro and scallions. Garnish with a sprinkling of chili powder and serve.

cook's tip

Serve the migas with sour cream on top, to melt seductively into the spicy eggs.

variation

Add browned ground beef or pork to the softly scrambling egg mixture. A bunch of cooked chopped spinach or chard can be stirred in as well, to add fresh color.

eggs oaxaca-style

serves 4

15 minutes

15 minutes

2 lb 4 oz/1 kg ripe tomatoes
about 12 pearl onions, halved
8 garlic cloves, whole and unpeeled
2 fresh mild green chiles
pinch of ground cumin
pinch of dried oregano
salt and pepper

pinch of sugar (optional)
2–3 tsp vegetable oil
8 eggs, lightly beaten
1–2 tbsp tomato paste
1–2 tbsp chopped fresh cilantro,
   to garnish

Cooking eggs in a flat omelet, then cutting them into strips and simmering them in a spicy sauce, makes an unusual dish for brunch or dinner.

Heat an unoiled heavy-based skillet. Add the tomatoes and char lightly, turning them once or twice. Remove from the skillet and let cool.

Meanwhile, lightly char the onions, garlic, and chiles in the skillet. Remove from the skillet and let cool slightly.

Cut the cooled tomatoes into pieces and place in a food processor or blender with their charred skins. Remove the stalks and seeds from the chiles, then peel and chop. Remove the skins from the garlic, then chop. Coarsely chop the onions. Add the chopped chiles, garlic, and onions to the tomatoes.

Process to make a coarse purée, then add the cumin and oregano. Season to taste with salt and pepper and add sugar, if necessary.

Heat the oil in a nonstick skillet. Add a ladleful of egg and cook to make a thin omelet. Continue to make omelets, stacking them on a plate as they are cooked. Slice into noodle-like ribbons.

Bring the sauce to a boil in a pan and adjust the seasoning, adding tomato paste to taste. Add the omelet strips, warm through, then serve at once, garnished with a sprinkling of cilantro.

eggs with refried beans

serves 4

15 minutes

25 minutes

14 oz/400 g tomatoes, peeled and chopped

1 onion, chopped

1 garlic clove, finely chopped

1/2 fresh green chile, such as jalapeño or serrano, seeded and chopped

1/4 tsp ground cumin

salt and pepper

2 tbsp virgin olive oil

1 plantain, peeled and diced

1 tbsp butter

4 soft corn tortillas, warmed or crisply fried into a tostada

about 14 oz/400 g canned refried beans, warmed with 2 tbsp water

2 tbsp butter or water

8 eggs

1 red bell pepper, broiled, peeled, seeded, and cut into strips

3–4 tbsp cooked peas, at room temperature

4–6 tbsp diced cooked or smoked ham

1/2–3/4 cup crumbled feta cheese

3 scallions, thinly sliced

In the Yucatan, this classic dish would be sandwiched between two crisp tortillas, but layering it all on top of one tortilla looks much more festive.

Place the tomatoes, onion, garlic, chile, cumin, and salt and pepper to taste in a food processor or blender and process to a purée.

Heat the oil in a heavy-bottomed skillet, then ladle in a little of the sauce and cook until it reduces in volume and becomes almost paste-like. Continue adding and reducing the sauce in this way. Keep warm.

Brown the plantain in the butter in a heavy-bottomed nonstick skillet. Remove and set aside. Spread the tortillas with the refried beans and keep warm in a low oven.

Heat the butter or water in the skillet, break in an egg, and cook until the white is set but the yolk is still soft. Remove from the skillet and place on top of one tortilla. Cook the remaining eggs in the same way, adding to the tortillas.

To serve, spoon the warm sauce around the eggs on each tortilla. Sprinkle over the diced plantain, red bell pepper, peas, ham, cheese, and scallions. Season to taste with salt and pepper and serve immediately.

fish with yucatan
flavors

serves 8

30 minutes,
plus 3 hours marinating

15 minutes

4 tbsp annatto seeds, soaked in water
   overnight
3 garlic cloves, finely chopped
1 tbsp mild chili powder
1 tbsp paprika
1 tsp ground cumin
½ tsp dried oregano
2 tbsp beer or tequila
juice of 1 lime and 1 orange or
   3 tbsp pineapple juice

2 tbsp olive oil
2 tbsp chopped fresh cilantro
¼ tsp ground cinnamon
¼ tsp ground cloves
2 lb 4 oz/1 kg swordfish steaks
banana leaves, for wrapping (optional)
fresh cilantro sprigs, to garnish
orange wedges, to serve

Annatto seeds are rock hard little red seeds that need to be soaked overnight before you can grind them. They have a distinctive lemony flavor and impart a dark orange color to the dish.

Drain the annatto, then crush them to a paste with a pestle and mortar. Work in the garlic, chili powder, paprika, cumin, oregano, beer, fruit juice, oil, cilantro, cinnamon, and cloves.

Smear the paste on to the fish, cover, and marinate in the refrigerator for at least 3 hours or overnight.

Wrap the fish steaks in banana leaves, tying with string to make pockets. Bring enough water to a boil in a steamer, then add a batch of pockets to the top part of the steamer and steam for 15 minutes, or until the fish is cooked through.

Alternatively, cook the fish without wrapping in the banana leaves. To cook on the grill, place in a hinged basket, or on a rack, and cook over hot coals for 5–6 minutes on each side, or until cooked through. Or cook the fish under a preheated hot broiler for 5–6 minutes on each side, or until cooked through.

Garnish with cilantro sprigs and serve with orange wedges for squeezing over the fish.

shrimp in green bean sauce

serves 4

10 minutes

20 minutes

2 tbsp vegetable oil

3 onions, chopped

5 garlic cloves, chopped

5–7 ripe tomatoes, diced

6–8 oz/175–225 g green beans, cut into 2-inch/5-cm pieces and blanched for 1 minute

¼ tsp ground cumin

pinch of ground allspice

pinch of ground cinnamon

½–1 canned chipotle chile in adobo marinade, with some of the marinade

2 cups fish stock or water mixed with 1 fish bouillon cube

1 lb/450 g raw shrimp, shelled and deveined

fresh cilantro sprigs, to garnish

1 lime, cut into wedges, to serve (optional)

The sweet briny flesh of shrimp is wonderful paired with the smoky scent of chipotle chile.

variation

If you can find them, use bottled nopales (edible cactus), cut into strips, to add an exotic touch to the dish.

Heat the oil in a large, deep skillet. Add the onions and garlic and cook over low heat for 5–10 minutes, or until softened. Add the tomatoes and cook for an additional 2 minutes.

Add the green beans, cumin, allspice, cinnamon, the chile and marinade, and stock. Bring to a boil, then reduce the heat and simmer for a few minutes to combine the flavors.

Add the shrimp and cook for 1–2 minutes only, then remove the skillet from the heat and let the shrimp steep in the hot liquid to finish cooking. They are cooked when they have turned a bright pink color.

Serve the shrimp immediately, garnished with the cilantro sprigs and accompanied by the lime wedges, if wished.

mussels cooked
with lager

serves 4

5–10 minutes

15 minutes

3 lb 5 oz/1.5 kg live mussels
2 cups lager
2 onions, chopped
5 garlic cloves, coarsely chopped
1 fresh green chile, such as jalapeño or serrano, seeded and thinly sliced

6 oz/175 g fresh tomatoes, diced, or canned, chopped
2–3 tbsp chopped fresh cilantro

Mussels cooked in beer, tomatoes, and Mexican spices are great summertime fare.

variation

Add the kernels of 2 corn cobs to the lager mixture in the second step. A pinch of sugar might be needed to bring out the sweetness of the corn.

Scrub the mussels under cold running water to remove any mud. Using a sharp knife, cut away the feathery "beards" from the shells. Discard any mussels with broken shells or any open mussels that do not shut when tapped sharply with a knife. Rinse again in cold water.

Place the lager, onions, garlic, chile, and tomatoes in a heavy-bottomed pan. Bring to a boil.

Add the mussels. Cook, covered, over medium–high heat for 10 minutes, or until the shells open. Discard any mussels that do not open.

Ladle into individual bowls and serve sprinkled with chopped cilantro.

grilled clams
with corn salsa

serves 4

5 minutes,
plus 30 minutes soaking

10 minutes

4 lb 8 oz/2 kg live clams in
  their shells
salt
5 ripe tomatoes
2 garlic cloves, finely chopped
8 oz/225 g canned corn, drained
3 tbsp finely chopped fresh cilantro
3 scallions, thinly sliced

¼ tsp ground cumin
juice of ½ lime
½–1 fresh green chile, seeded and
  finely chopped
fresh cilantro sprig, to garnish
lime wedges, to serve

*Cook with Mexican flair and
serve up clams from the
barbecue topped with
a spicy corn salsa.*

variation

*Mussels can be used in place
of the clams very successfully.*

Preheat the grill. Place the clams in a large bowl. Cover with cold water and add a handful of salt. Let soak for 30 minutes to rinse out the sand and grit.

Meanwhile, peel the tomatoes. Place in a heatproof bowl, pour boiling water over to cover, and let stand for 30 seconds. Drain and plunge into cold water. The skins will then slide off easily. Cut the tomatoes in half, seed, then chop the flesh.

To make the salsa, combine the tomatoes, garlic, corn, cilantro, scallions, cumin, lime juice, and chile in a nonmetallic bowl. Season to taste with salt.

Drain the clams, discarding any that are open. Place the clams on the hot coals of the grill and cook for 5 minutes per side, or until they pop open. Discard any that do not open.

Immediately remove from the grill, top with the salsa, and garnish with cilantro. Serve with lime wedges for squeezing over the clams.

chili-marinated shrimp
with avocado sauce

serves 4

15 minutes

5 minutes

1 lb 7 oz/650 g large raw shrimp, shelled, deveined, and tails left intact

½ tsp ground cumin

½ tsp mild chili powder

½ tsp paprika

2 tbsp orange juice

grated rind of 1 orange

2 tbsp extra-virgin olive oil

2 tbsp chopped fresh cilantro, plus extra to garnish

salt and pepper

2 ripe avocados

½ onion, finely chopped

¼ fresh green or red chile, seeded and chopped

juice of ½ lime

Avocado salsa is delicious spooned on to anything spicy from the broiler or grill, especially seafood.

variation

For luscious sandwiches, toast crusty rolls, cut in half and buttered, over the hot coals and fill them with the cooked shrimp and avocado sauce.

Preheat the grill. Combine the shrimp with the cumin, chili powder, paprika, orange juice and rind, oil, and half the cilantro. Season to taste with salt and pepper.

Thread the shrimp on to metal skewers, or bamboo skewers that have been soaked in cold water for 30 minutes.

Cut the avocados in half around the pit. Twist apart, then remove the pit with a knife. Carefully peel off the skin, then dice the flesh. Immediately combine the avocados with the remaining cilantro, onion, chile, and lime juice in a nonmetallic bowl. Season to taste with salt and pepper and set aside.

Place the shrimp over the hot coals of the grill and cook for only a few minutes on each side, or until bright pink and opaque.

Serve the shrimp garnished with chopped cilantro and accompanied by the avocado sauce.

squid simmered with
tomatoes & olives

serves 4

10 minutes

20 minutes

3 tbsp virgin olive oil

2 lb/900 g cleaned squid, cut into rings and tentacles

salt and pepper

1 onion, chopped

3 garlic cloves, chopped

14 oz/400 g canned chopped tomatoes

1/2–1 fresh mild to medium green chile, seeded and chopped

1 tbsp finely chopped fresh parsley

1/4 tsp chopped fresh thyme

1/4 tsp chopped fresh oregano

1/4 tsp chopped fresh marjoram

large pinch of ground cinnamon

large pinch of ground allspice

large pinch of sugar

15–20 pimiento-stuffed green olives, sliced

1 tbsp capers

1 tbsp chopped fresh cilantro, to garnish

This flavorful squid dish from Veracruz would be good with warmed flour tortillas, for do-it-yourself tacos.

Heat the oil in a deep, heavy-bottomed skillet. Add the squid and lightly cook until it turns opaque. Season to taste with salt and pepper and remove from the skillet with a slotted spoon. Set aside in a bowl.

Add the onion and garlic to the remaining oil in the skillet and cook for 5 minutes, or until softened. Stir in the tomatoes, chile, herbs, cinnamon, allspice, sugar, and olives. Cover and cook over medium–low heat for 5–10 minutes, or until the mixture thickens slightly. Uncover the skillet and cook for an additional 5 minutes to concentrate the flavors.

Stir in the reserved squid and any of the juices that have gathered in the bowl. Add the capers and heat through.

Adjust the seasoning, then serve immediately, garnished with cilantro.

pan-fried scallops mexicana

serves 4–6

5 minutes

10 minutes

2 tbsp butter
2 tbsp virgin olive oil
1 lb 7 oz/650 g scallops, shelled
4–5 scallions, thinly sliced
3–4 garlic cloves, finely chopped
½ fresh green chile, seeded and finely chopped

2 tbsp finely chopped fresh cilantro
½ lime
salt and pepper
lime wedges, to serve

Scallops, with their sweet flesh, are delicious with the citrus flavors of Mexico. Often they are prepared just this simply, served with wedges of lime to squeeze over as desired, and a stack of warm corn tortillas.

variation

Mix leftover scallops with a little aïoli or mayonnaise mixed with garlic and a little olive oil. Serve with roasted bell peppers on a bed of greens, with a handful of salty black olives for a taste of the Mediterranean, Mexico-style.

Heat half the butter and oil in a large, heavy-bottomed skillet until the butter foams.

Add the scallops and cook quickly until just turning opaque; do not over-cook. Remove from the skillet with a slotted spoon and keep warm.

Add the remaining butter and oil to the skillet, then toss in the scallions and garlic and cook over medium heat until the scallions are wilted. Return the scallops to the skillet.

Remove the skillet from the heat and add the chile and cilantro. Squeeze in the lime juice. Season to taste with salt and pepper and stir to mix well.

Serve immediately with lime wedges for squeezing over the scallops.

spicy broiled salmon

serves 4

15 minutes,
plus 1 hour marinating

8 minutes

4 salmon steaks, about 6–8 oz/
175–225 g each

marinade

4 garlic cloves

2 tbsp extra-virgin olive oil

pinch of ground allspice

pinch of ground cinnamon

juice of 2 limes

1–2 tsp marinade from canned
chipotle chiles or bottled chipotle
chili salsa

1/4 tsp ground cumin

pinch of sugar

salt and pepper

lime slices, to garnish

to serve

tomato wedges

3 scallions, finely chopped

shredded lettuce

*The woody smoked flavors of
the chipotle chile are delicious
brushed on to salmon
for broiling.*

To make the marinade, finely chop the garlic and place in a nonmetallic bowl with the oil, allspice, cinnamon, lime juice, chipotle marinade, cumin, and sugar. Add salt and pepper to taste and stir to combine.

Coat the salmon with the garlic mixture, then transfer to a large nonmetallic dish. Cover with plastic wrap and let marinate in the refrigerator for 1 hour.

Preheat the broiler to medium. Transfer the salmon to a broiler pan and cook under the hot broiler for 3–4 minutes on each side, or until cooked through. Alternatively, cook the salmon over hot coals on a grill until cooked through.

variation

*The marinade also goes well
with fresh tuna steaks.*

To serve, mix the tomato wedges with the scallions. Place the salmon on individual plates and arrange the tomato salad and shredded lettuce alongside. Garnish with lime slices and serve immediately.

fish baked with lime

serves 4

15 minutes

20 minutes

2 lb 4 oz/1 kg white fish fillets, such
    as bass, flounder, or cod

salt and pepper

1 lime, halved

3 tbsp virgin olive oil

1 large onion, finely chopped

3 garlic cloves, finely chopped

2–3 pickled jalapeño chiles (see
    Cook's Tip), chopped, plus extra
    whole chiles to serve (optional)

6–8 tbsp chopped fresh cilantro

lemon and lime wedges, to serve

*Tangy and simple to prepare,
this is excellent served with rice
and beans for an easy lunch.
Follow up with coffee ice cream
topped with espresso beans and
chocolate sauce.*

Preheat the oven to 350°F/180°C. Place the fish fillets in a nonmetallic
bowl and sprinkle with salt and pepper to taste. Squeeze the juice from
the lime over the fish.

Heat the oil in a skillet. Add the onion and garlic and cook for 2 minutes,
or until softened, stirring frequently. Remove from the heat.

Place a third of the onion mixture and a little of the chiles and cilantro in
the bottom of a shallow baking dish or roasting pan. Arrange the fish on
top. Top with the remaining onion mixture, chiles, and coriander.

Bake in the oven for 15–20 minutes, or until the fish has become slightly
opaque and firm to the touch. Serve at once, with lemon and lime wedges
for squeezing over the fish and whole pickled chiles, if wished.

cook's tip

*Pickled jalapeño chiles are
called jalapeño chiles en
escabeche and are available
from specialty markets.*

variation

*Add sliced flavorful fresh tomatoes,
or canned chopped tomatoes, to
the onion mixture at the end of
the second step.*

lobster cooked rosarita beach-style

serves 4

10 minutes

15 minutes

2–4 cooked lobsters, depending on their size, cut through the middle into halves, or 4 lobster tails, the meat loosened slightly from the shells

chili butter

½ cup unsalted butter, softened

3–4 tbsp chopped fresh cilantro

about 5 garlic cloves, chopped

2–3 tbsp mild chili powder

juice of ½ lime

salt and pepper

to serve

14 oz/400 g canned refried beans, warmed with 2 tbsp water

chopped scallions

lime wedges

salsa of your choice

Grilling gives lobsters a lovely smoky scent that is enhanced by spicy red chili. Serve with creamy refried beans and a stack of warmed corn tortillas and pretend you're on Rosarita Beach in Baja California!

cook's tip

The flavored butter is also delicious with broiled fish steaks and large shrimp.

Preheat the grill. To make the chilli butter, place the butter in a small non-metallic bowl and mix in the cilantro, garlic, chili powder, and lime juice. Add salt and pepper to taste.

Rub the butter mixture into the cut side of the lobsters or the lobster tails, working it into all the lobsters' cracks and crevices.

Wrap loosely in foil and place, cut-side up, on a rack over the hot coals of the grill. Cook for 15 minutes, or until heated through.

Serve with warmed refried beans, topped with chopped scallions, plus lime wedges and salsa.

ropa vieja

serves 6

15 minutes,
plus 30 minutes cooling

2 hours 15 minutes

3 lb 5 oz/1 ½ kg flank beef steak or
  other stewing meat

beef stock

1 carrot, sliced

10 garlic cloves, sliced

salt and pepper

2 tbsp vegetable oil

2 onions, thinly sliced

3–4 mild fresh green chiles, such as
  Anaheim or poblano, seeded
  and sliced

warmed flour tortillas, to serve

salad garnishes

3 ripe tomatoes, diced

8–10 radishes, diced

3–4 tbsp chopped fresh cilantro

4–5 scallions, chopped

1–2 limes, cut into wedges

Fill warmed tortillas with this tender, browned beef and a selection of crisp vegetables to make wonderful tacos.

Place the meat in a large pan and cover with a mixture of stock and water. Add the carrot and half the garlic with salt and pepper to taste. Cover and bring to a boil, then reduce the heat to low. Skim the scum that rises to the surface, then re-cover the pan and cook the meat gently for 2 hours, or until very tender.

Remove the pan from the heat and let the meat cool in the liquid. When cool enough to handle, remove from the liquid and shred with your fingers and a fork.

Heat the oil in a large, heavy-bottomed skillet. Add the remaining garlic, onions, and chiles and cook until lightly colored. Remove from the skillet and set aside.

Add the meat to the skillet and cook over medium–high heat until browned and crisp. Transfer to a serving dish. Top with the onion mixture and surround with the tomatoes, radishes, cilantro, scallions, and lime wedges. Serve with warmed tortillas.

classic beef fajitas

serves 4–6

15 minutes,
plus 30 minutes marinating

20 minutes

1 lb 9 oz/700 g sirloin steak or other
   tender beef steak, cut into strips

6 garlic cloves, chopped

juice of 1 lime

large pinch of mild chili powder

large pinch of paprika

large pinch of ground cumin

1–2 tbsp extra-virgin olive oil

salt and pepper

12 flour tortillas

vegetable oil, for oiling and frying

1–2 avocados, pitted, peeled, diced,
   and tossed with lime juice

¼ cup sour cream

pico de gallo salsa

8 ripe tomatoes, diced

3 scallions, sliced

1–2 fresh green chiles, such as
   jalapeño or serrano, seeded
   and chopped

3–4 tbsp chopped fresh cilantro

5–8 radishes, diced

ground cumin, to taste

salt and pepper

*Sizzling marinated strips of meat
rolled up in soft flour tortillas with a
tangy salsa is a real Mexican treat,
perfect for relaxed entertaining.*

Combine the strips of steak with half the garlic and lime juice, the chili
powder, paprika, cumin, and oil. Add salt and pepper to taste and mix well.
Cover and let marinate for at least 30 minutes at room temperature, or
overnight in the refrigerator.

To make the pico de gallo salsa, place the tomatoes in a bowl with the
scallions, chiles, cilantro, and radishes. Season to taste with cumin, salt, and
pepper. Set aside.

Heat the tortillas in a lightly oiled nonstick skillet; wrap in foil or a clean
dish towel as you work to keep them warm.

cook's tip

*A lettuce and orange salad makes
a refreshing accompaniment.*

Heat a little oil in a large skillet or preheated wok. Add the beef and stir-fry
over high heat until browned and just cooked through.

Serve the sizzling hot meat with the warmed tortillas, salsa, avocado, and
sour cream for each person to make his or her own rolled-up fajitas.

michoacan beef

serves 4–6

10 minutes

2 hours

about 3 tbsp all-purpose flour

salt and pepper

2 lb 4 oz/1 kg stewing beef, cut into large bite-size pieces

2 tbsp vegetable oil

2 onions, chopped

5 garlic cloves, chopped

14 oz/400 g tomatoes, diced

1 1/2 dried chipotle chiles, reconstituted (see page 100), seeded, and cut into thin strips, or a few shakes of bottled chipotle salsa

1 1/4 quarts beef stock

12 oz/350 g green beans

pinch of sugar

to serve

simmered beans

freshly cooked rice

This rich smoky flavored stew is delicious; leftovers make a great filling for tacos, too!

cook's tip

This is traditionally made with nopales, edible cactus, which gives the dish a distinctive flavor. Look out for them in specialty markets. For this recipe you need 12–14 oz/350–400 g canned nopales, or fresh nopales, peeled, sliced, and blanched. Add them to the stew with the tomatoes.

Place the flour in a large bowl and season to taste with salt and pepper. Add the beef and toss to coat well. Remove the beef from the bowl, shaking off the excess flour.

Heat the oil in a skillet. Add the beef and brown briefly over high heat. Reduce the heat to medium, add the onions and garlic, and cook for 2 minutes.

Add the tomatoes, chiles, and stock, then cover and simmer over low heat for 1 1/2 hours, or until the meat is very tender, adding the green beans and sugar 15 minutes before the end of the cooking time. Skim off any fat that rises to the surface every now and again.

Transfer to individual bowls and serve with simmered beans and rice.

chiles stuffed with beef

serves 4

15 minutes,
plus 20 minutes standing

30–40 minutes

4 large fresh poblano chiles
all-purpose flour, for dusting
vegetable oil, for frying

spicy beef filling

1 lb 2 oz/500 g ground beef
1 onion, finely chopped
2–3 garlic cloves, finely chopped
4 tbsp dry or sweet sherry
pinch of ground cinnamon
pinch of ground cloves
pinch of ground cumin
salt and pepper
14 oz/400 g canned chopped tomatoes

1–3 tsp sugar
1 tbsp vinegar
3 tbsp chopped fresh cilantro
2–3 tbsp coarsely chopped toasted
  almonds

batter

3 eggs, separated
6–8 tbsp all-purpose flour
pinch of salt
about ½ cup water

Quick Tomato Sauce (see page 83),
  to serve

*Large, mildish-tasting green chiles
are roasted, peeled, and stuffed
with a succulent meat mixture
that is sweet, spicy, and
punctuated with nuts.*

Preheat the broiler to medium. Roast the chiles under the hot broiler until
the skin is charred. Place in a plastic bag, twist to seal well, and let stand for
20 minutes. Make a slit in the side of each chile and remove the seeds,
leaving the stalks intact. Set aside.

To make the filling, brown the meat and onion together in a heavy-
bottomed skillet over medium heat. Pour off any extra fat, then add the
garlic and sherry and boil down until the liquid has nearly evaporated.

Add the cinnamon, cloves, cumin, and salt and pepper to taste. Stir in the
tomatoes, sugar, and vinegar and cook over medium heat until the
tomatoes have reduced to a thick, strongly flavored sauce.

Stir in the cilantro and almonds and heat through. Stuff as much of the
filling into the chiles as will fit, then dust each with flour. Set aside.

To make the batter, in a large bowl, lightly beat the egg yolks with the flour,
salt, and enough of the water to make a thick mixture. In a separate bowl,
whisk the egg whites until they form stiff peaks. Fold the egg whites into
the batter, then gently dip each stuffed chile into the batter.

Heat the oil in a deep skillet until very hot and just smoking. Add the
chiles and fry until they are golden brown. Serve hot, topped with the
Quick Tomato Sauce.

spicy pork with prunes

serves 4–6

15 minutes,
plus 8 hours marinating

3–4 hours

1 pork joint, such as leg or shoulder,
   weighing 3 lb 5 oz/1.5 kg

juice of 2–3 limes

10 garlic cloves, chopped

3–4 tbsp mild chili powder, such as
   ancho or New Mexico

4 tbsp vegetable oil

salt

2 onions, chopped

2¼ cups chicken stock

25 small tart tomatoes, coarsely
   chopped

25 prunes, pitted

1–2 tsp sugar

pinch of ground cinnamon

pinch of ground allspice

pinch of ground cumin

warmed corn tortillas, to serve

Prunes add an earthy, wine flavor to this spicy stew. Serve with tortillas or crusty bread to dip into the rich sauce.

Combine the pork with the lime juice, garlic, chili powder, half the oil, and salt to taste in a nonmetallic bowl or dish. Cover and let marinate in the refrigerator overnight.

Preheat the oven to 350°F/180°C. Remove the pork from the marinade. Wipe the pork dry with paper towels and reserve the marinade. Heat the remaining oil in a flameproof casserole and brown the pork evenly until just golden. Add the onions, the reserved marinade, and stock. Cover and cook in the oven for 2–3 hours, or until tender.

Remove the casserole from the oven and spoon off the fat from the surface of the cooking liquid. Add the tomatoes. Return to the oven for 20 minutes, or until the tomatoes are tender. Remove the casserole from the oven. Mash the tomatoes into a coarse purée. Add the prunes and sugar, then adjust the seasoning, adding cinnamon, allspice, and cumin, as well as extra chili powder, if wished.

Increase the oven temperature to 400°F/200°C and return the casserole to the oven for an additional 20–30 minutes, or until the meat has browned on top and the juices have thickened.

Remove the meat from the casserole and let stand for a few minutes. Carefully carve the joint into thin slices and spoon the sauce over the top. Serve warm, with corn tortillas.

mole of pork & red chiles

serves 6

15 minutes

4 hours

2 lb 12 oz/1 ¼ kg pork shoulder or
   lean belly, cut into bite-size pieces

1 onion, chopped

1 whole garlic bulb

2 bay leaves

salt and pepper

1–2 bouillon cubes

6 dried ancho chiles

6 guajillo chiles or, if unavailable,
   de agua chiles

3–5 large ripe flavorful tomatoes

¼ tsp ground cloves

¼ tsp ground allspice

¾ cup sesame seeds, toasted

1 large ripe plantain or banana,
   peeled and diced

3 tbsp vegetable oil

6–8 waxy potatoes, cut into chunks

3 tbsp yerba santa or, if unavailable,
   a combination of chopped fresh
   mint, oregano, and cilantro,
   plus a sprig to garnish

1 cinnamon stick

*Plantain and sesame seeds
add a delicious hint of sweetness
to this fragrant stew of pork and
chiles, while potatoes add a
satisfying chunky texture.*

Place the pork in a large flameproof casserole with the onion, garlic, bay leaves, and salt and pepper to taste. Fill with cold water to the top.

Bring to a boil, then reduce the heat to a slow simmer. Skim off the scum that rises to the surface, then stir in the bouillon cubes. Cook, covered, for 3 hours, or until the pork is very tender.

Meanwhile, lightly roast the chiles in an unoiled heavy-bottomed skillet until they just change color. Place them in a heatproof bowl and cover with boiling water. Cover and let soften for 20–30 minutes.

Preheat the broiler to medium. Roast the tomatoes in the skillet to brown the bottoms, then char the tops under the hot broiler. Let cool.

When the chiles are softened, remove the stalks and seeds, transfer to a food processor or blender, and process with enough liquid to form a paste. Add the roasted tomatoes, cloves, allspice, two-thirds of the sesame seeds, and the plantain and process until smooth.

Remove the meat from the pan and reserve. Skim the fat from the surface of the stock.

Heat the oil in a separate pan. Add the tomato mixture and cook for 10 minutes, or until thickened. Add the potatoes and herbs with enough of the stock to keep the potatoes covered in sauce. Add the cinnamon stick. Cook, covered, until the potatoes are tender. Add the reserved pork and heat through. Serve in bowls, sprinkled with the remaining sesame seeds.

chile verde

serves 4

15 minutes

2 hours

2 lb 4 oz/1 kg pork, cut into bite-size chunks

1 onion, chopped

2 bay leaves

1 whole garlic bulb, cut in half

1 bouillon cube

2 garlic cloves, chopped

1 lb oz/450 g fresh tomatillos, husks removed, cooked in a small amount of water until just tender, then chopped, or canned

2 large fresh mild green chiles, such as Anaheim, or a combination of 1 green bell pepper and 2 jalapeño chiles, seeded and chopped

3 tbsp vegetable oil

½ cup pork or chicken stock

½ tsp mild chili powder, such as ancho or New Mexico

½ tsp ground cumin

4–6 tbsp chopped fresh cilantro, to garnish

to serve

warmed flour tortillas

lime wedges

If tomatillos are not available, use fresh tomatoes and bottled green salsa instead, and add a good hit of lime juice at the end.

Place the pork in a large, flameproof casserole with the onion, bay leaves, and garlic bulb. Add water to cover and the bouillon cube and bring to a boil. Skim off the scum that rises to the surface, reduce the heat to very low, and simmer gently for 1½ hours, or until the meat is very tender.

Meanwhile, place the chopped garlic in a food processor or blender with the tomatillos, chiles, and green bell pepper, if using. Process to a purée.

Heat the oil in a deep skillet. Add the tomatillo mixture and cook over medium–high heat for 10 minutes, or until thickened. Add the stock, chili powder, and cumin.

When the meat is tender, remove from the casserole and add to the sauce. Simmer gently for 20 minutes, or until the flavors are combined.

Garnish with the chopped cilantro and serve with warmed tortillas and lime wedges.

meatballs in
spicy-sweet sauce

serves 4

20 minutes

20 minutes

8 oz/225 g ground pork

8 oz/225 g ground beef or lamb

6 tbsp cooked rice or finely crushed tortilla chips

1 egg, lightly beaten

1½ onions, finely chopped

5 garlic cloves, finely chopped

½ tsp ground cumin

large pinch of ground cinnamon

2 tbsp raisins

1 tbsp molasses sugar

1–2 tbsp cider or wine vinegar

14 oz/400 g canned tomatoes, drained and chopped

1½ cups beef stock

1–2 tbsp mild chili or ancho chili powder

1 tbsp paprika

1 tbsp chopped fresh cilantro

1 tbsp chopped fresh parsley or mint

2 tbsp vegetable oil, plus extra if needed

2 sweet potatoes, peeled and cut into small bite-size chunks

salt and pepper

to serve

grated cheese

lightly cooked green beans (optional)

Called albondigas *in Mexico, these tasty meatballs are set off brilliantly against the rich sauce and golden sweet potatoes.*

Mix the meat thoroughly with the rice or crushed tortilla chips, the egg, half the onion and garlic, the cumin, cinnamon, and raisins.

Divide the mixture into even-size pieces and roll into balls. Fry the balls in a nonstick skillet over medium heat, adding a little oil, if necessary, to help them brown. Remove the balls from the skillet and set aside. Wipe the skillet clean.

Place the sugar in a food processor or blender with the vinegar, tomatoes, stock, chili powder, paprika, and remaining onion and garlic. Process until blended, then stir in the herbs. Set aside.

Heat the oil in the cleaned skillet. Add the sweet potatoes and cook until tender and golden brown. Pour in the blended sauce and add the meatballs to the skillet. Cook for 10 minutes, or until the meatballs are heated through and the flavors have combined. Season to taste with salt and pepper. Serve with grated cheese and green beans, if wished.

carnitas

serves 4–6

15 minutes,
plus 30 minutes cooling

2 hours 30 minutes

2 lb 4 oz/1 kg pork, such as lean belly
1 onion, chopped
1 whole garlic bulb, cut in half
½ tsp ground cumin
2 meat bouillon cubes
2 bay leaves
salt and pepper
fresh chile strips, to garnish

to serve

freshly cooked rice
Refried Beans (see page 145)
   or canned
salsa of your choice

In this classic Mexican dish, pieces of pork are first simmered to make them meltingly tender, then browned until irresistibly crisp.

Place the pork in a heavy-bottomed pan with the onion, garlic, cumin, bouillon cubes, and bay leaves. Add water to cover. Bring to a boil, then reduce the heat to very low. Skim off the scum that rises to the surface.

Continue to cook very gently for 2 hours, or until the pork is tender. Remove from the heat and let the pork cool in the liquid.

Remove the pork from the pan with a slotted spoon. Cut off any skin (roast separately to make crackling). Cut the pork into bite-size pieces and sprinkle with salt and pepper to taste. Reserve 1¼ cups of the cooking liquid.

Brown the pork in a heavy-bottomed skillet for 15 minutes, to cook out the fat. Add the reserved cooking liquid and allow to reduce down. Continue to cook the meat for 15 minutes, covering the skillet to avoid splattering. Turn the pork every now and again.

Transfer the pork to a serving dish, garnish with chile strips, and serve with rice, Refried Beans, and salsa.

spicy meat & chipotle hash

serves 6

10 minutes

20 minutes

1 tbsp vegetable oil

1 onion, finely chopped

1 lb/450 g leftover meat, such as simmered pork or beef, cooled and cut into thin strips

1 tbsp mild chili powder

2 ripe tomatoes, seeded and diced

about 1 cup meat stock

½–1 canned chipotle chile, mashed, plus a little of the marinade, or a few shakes of bottled chipotle salsa

chopped fresh cilantro, plus extra to serve

to serve

warmed soft corn tortillas

½ cup sour cream

4–6 tbsp chopped radishes

3–4 crisp lettuce leaves, such as romaine, shredded

This specialty from the town of Puebla in Mexico makes divine soft tacos: simply serve with a stack of warmed soft corn tortillas and let everyone roll their own, fajita-style.

cook's tip

Avocados add an interesting texture contrast to the spicy meat—serve with 2 sliced avocados, tossed with lime juice. Try serving on top of tostadas—crisply fried tortillas—instead of wrapping taco-style.

Heat the oil in a skillet. Add the onion and cook until softened, stirring occasionally. Add the meat and cook for about 3 minutes, or until lightly browned, stirring.

Add the chili powder, tomatoes, and stock and cook until the tomatoes reduce to a sauce; mash the meat a little as it cooks.

Add the chile and continue to cook and mash until the sauce and meat are nearly blended.

Serve the dish, garnished with chopped cilantro, with a stack of warmed corn tortillas so that people can fill them with the meaty mixture to make tacos. Also serve sour cream, additional cilantro, radishes, and lettuce for each person to add to the meat.

stew of meat, chicken, vegetables & fruits

serves 6–8

10 minutes

2 hours 15 minutes

2 lb/900 g boneless pork, either in one joint or in pieces

2 bay leaves

1 onion, chopped

8 garlic cloves, finely chopped

2 tbsp chopped fresh cilantro

1 carrot, thinly sliced

2 celery stalks, diced

2 chicken bouillon cubes

1/2 chicken, cut into portions

4–5 ripe tomatoes, diced

1/2 tsp mild chili powder

grated rind of 1/4 orange

1/4 tsp ground cumin

juice of 3 oranges

1 zucchini, cut into bite-size pieces

1/4 cabbage, thinly sliced and blanched

1 apple, cut into bite-size pieces

about 10 prunes, pitted

1/4 tsp ground cinnamon

pinch of ground ginger

2 hard chorizo sausages, about 12 oz/350 g in total, cut into bite-size pieces

salt and pepper

A big pot of cocido is warming on a cold day—great for a family meal. Serve with a selection of several salsas, a stack of corn tortillas, and a bowl of rice.

Combine the pork, bay leaves, onion, garlic, cilantro, carrot, and celery in a flameproof casserole and fill with cold water. Bring to a boil and skim off the scum that rises to surface. Reduce the heat and simmer for 1 hour.

Add the bouillon cubes to the casserole, along with the chicken, tomatoes, chili powder, orange rind, and cumin. Continue to cook for an additional 45 minutes, or until the chicken is tender. Spoon off the fat that forms on the top of the liquid.

Add the orange juice, zucchini, cabbage, apple, prunes, cinnamon, ginger, and chorizo. Continue to simmer for an additional 20 minutes, or until the zucchini is soft and tender and the chorizo is cooked through.

Season the stew to taste with salt and pepper. Serve immediately.

chicken breasts in green
salsa with sour cream

serves 4

10 minutes

25 minutes

4 chicken breast fillets

salt and pepper

all-purpose flour, for dredging

2–3 tbsp butter or a combination of butter and oil

1 lb/450 g mild green salsa or puréed tomatillos

1 cup chicken stock

1–2 garlic cloves, finely chopped

3–5 tbsp chopped fresh cilantro

1/2 fresh green chile, seeded and chopped

1/2 tsp ground cumin

to serve

1 cup sour cream

several romaine lettuce leaves, shredded

3–5 scallions, thinly sliced

coarsely chopped fresh cilantro

Chicken breasts bathed in a fragrant sauce make a delicate dish, perfect for dinner parties. Serve with rice to complete the meal.

Sprinkle the chicken with salt and pepper to taste, then dredge in flour. Shake off the excess.

Melt the butter in a skillet, add the chicken breasts, and cook over medium –high heat, turning once, until they are golden but not cooked through—they will continue to cook in the sauce. Remove the chicken from the skillet and set aside.

Place the salsa, stock, garlic, cilantro, chile, and cumin in a pan and bring to a boil. Reduce the heat to a low simmer. Add the chicken to the sauce, spooning the sauce over the chicken. Cook for 25–30 minutes, or until the chicken is cooked through and tender.

Remove the chicken from the pan and season to taste with salt and pepper. Serve with the sour cream, shredded lettuce, sliced scallions, and chopped cilantro.

chicken with yucatan vinegar sauce

serves 4–6

15 minutes,
plus 30 minutes standing

35–45 minutes

8 small boned chicken thighs
chicken stock
15–20 garlic cloves, unpeeled
1 tsp coarsely ground black pepper
1/2 tsp ground cloves
2 tsp crumbled dried oregano or
1/2 tsp crushed bay leaves
about 1/2 tsp salt
1 tbsp lime juice
1 tsp cumin seeds, lightly toasted

1 tbsp all-purpose flour, plus extra
for dredging
1/2 cup vegetable oil
3–4 onions, thinly sliced
2 fresh chiles, preferably mild yellow
ones, such as Mexican Guero or
similar Turkish or Greek chiles,
seeded and sliced
generous 1/3 cup cider or sherry
vinegar

A paste of roasted garlic and mixed spices gives an evocative flavor to this tangy dish of simmered chicken, a specialty of Valladolid in the Yucatan peninsula.

Place the chicken in a pan with enough stock to cover. Bring to a boil, then reduce the heat and simmer for 5 minutes. Remove from the heat and let the chicken continue to cook while cooling in the stock.

Meanwhile, roast the garlic in an unoiled heavy-bottomed, nonstick skillet until the cloves are lightly browned on all sides and tender inside. Remove from the heat. When cool enough to handle, squeeze the flesh from the skins and place in a bowl.

Using a pestle and mortar, grind the garlic with the pepper, cloves, oregano, salt, lime juice, and three-quarters of the cumin seeds. Mix with the flour.

Remove the chicken from the stock, reserving the stock, and pat dry. Rub with two-thirds of the spice paste. Cover and let stand at room temperature for at least 30 minutes or overnight in the refrigerator.

Heat a little of the oil in a skillet and cook the onions and chiles until golden brown and softened. Pour in the vinegar and remaining cumin seeds, cook for a few minutes, then add the reserved stock and remaining spice paste. Boil, stirring, for 10 minutes, or until reduced in volume.

Dredge the chicken in flour. Heat the remaining oil in a heavy-bottomed skillet. Fry the chicken until lightly browned and the juices run clear when a skewer is inserted into the thickest part. Serve topped with the sauce.

tequila-marinated crisp
chicken wings

serves 4

10 minutes,
plus 3 hours marinating

15–20 minutes

2 lb/900 g chicken wings
11 garlic cloves, finely chopped
juice of 2 limes
juice of 1 orange
2 tbsp tequila
1 tbsp mild chili powder
2 tsp Chipotle Salsa (see page 99)
   or 2 dried chipotle chiles,
   reconstituted (see page 100)
   and puréed

2 tbsp vegetable oil
1 tsp sugar
1/4 tsp ground allspice
pinch of ground cinnamon
pinch of ground cumin
pinch of dried oregano
grilled or broiled tomato halves, to
   serve (optional)

The tequila tenderizes these tasty chicken wings and gives them a delicious flavor. Serve as part of a barbecue, accompanied by corn tortillas, refried beans, salsa, and lots of chilled lager.

Cut the chicken wings into 2 pieces at the joint.

Place the chicken wings in a nonmetallic dish and add the remaining ingredients. Toss well to coat, then cover and let marinate in the refrigerator for at least 3 hours or overnight.

Preheat the grill. Cook the chicken wings over the hot coals of the grill for 15–20 minutes, or until crisply browned and the juices run clear when a skewer is inserted into the thickest part of the meat, turning occasionally. Alternatively, cook in a ridged grill pan. Serve at once, with grilled or broiled tomato halves, if wished.

citrus-marinated chicken

serves 4

15 minutes,
plus 1 hour marinating

25 minutes

1 chicken, cut into 4 pieces
1 tbsp mild chili powder
1 tbsp paprika
2 tsp ground cumin
juice and rind of 1 orange
juice of 3 limes
pinch of sugar
8–10 garlic cloves, finely chopped
1 bunch fresh cilantro, coarsely
  chopped

2–3 tbsp extra-virgin olive oil
4 tbsp beer, tequila, or pineapple juice
  (optional)
salt and pepper
fresh cilantro sprigs, to garnish

to serve

lime wedges
tomato, green bell pepper, and
  scallion salad

This is a great dish for a summer meal. The marinade gives the chicken an appetizing flavor and helps keeps it succulent and moist during cooking.

Place the chicken in a nonmetallic dish. Mix the remaining ingredients together in a bowl and season to taste with salt and pepper.

Pour over the chicken, turn to coat well, then cover and let marinate for at least an hour at room temperature. If possible, leave for 24 hours in the refrigerator to marinate.

Preheat the broiler to medium. Remove the chicken from the marinade and pat dry with paper towels.

Place the chicken on a broiler pan and cook under the hot broiler for 20–25 minutes, turning once, until the chicken is tender and the juices run clear when a skewer is inserted into the thickest part of the meat. Alternatively, cook in a ridged grill pan. Brush with the marinade occasionally, but not for the last few minutes of the cooking time.

Garnish with cilantro sprigs and serve with lime wedges and a tomato, green bell pepper, and scallion salad.

squab chickens in marinade

serves 4

15 minutes,
plus 3 hours marinating

20 minutes

10 garlic cloves, chopped

juice of 1 lime

1 bunch fresh cilantro, finely chopped

½ fresh green chile, seeded and chopped

1 tsp ground cumin

4 squab chickens

1½ cups sour cream

1 red bell pepper, roasted, peeled, seeded, and diced

¼–1 tsp marinade from chipotle chiles canned in adobo marinade or chipotle salsa

salt and pepper

3–5 scallions, thinly sliced

handful of toasted pumpkin seeds

Flavored with a green herb marinade, these elegant squab chickens are packed with lively Mexican flavors.

variation

For barbecued lamb, skewer lamb chunks, such as shoulder or leg, on to metal or pre-soaked bamboo skewers. Marinate in the green herb marinade as in the first step, then cook over the hot coals of a grill until the lamb is cooked to your liking.

Combine about 9 garlic cloves with the lime juice, about three-quarters of the cilantro, the chile, and half the cumin in a nonmetallic bowl. Press the mixture on to the chickens, cover, and let marinate for at least 3 hours in the refrigerator or preferably overnight.

Preheat the oven to 400°F/200°C. Place the chickens in a roasting pan and roast in the oven for 15 minutes. Remove one from the oven at this point to check whether it is cooked—pierce the thigh with a knife and if the juices run clear, the chicken is cooked. If necessary, return to the oven and continue to roast until cooked through.

Meanwhile, mix the sour cream with the red bell pepper, chipotle marinade, and remaining garlic and cumin. Season to taste with salt and pepper.

Serve each chicken immediately with a spoonful of the bell pepper sauce and a sprinkling of the remaining cilantro, the scallions, and the toasted pumpkin seeds.

chicken with
purslane & chile

serves 4

15 minutes, plus 1 hour 30 minutes marinating/standing

1 hour

juice of 1 lime
6 garlic cloves, finely chopped
¼ tsp dried oregano
¼ tsp dried marjoram
¼ tsp dried thyme
½ tsp ground cumin
salt and pepper
1 chicken, cut into 4 pieces
about 10 large dried mild chiles, such as pasilla, toasted
2 cups boiling water

2 cups chicken stock
3 tbsp virgin olive oil
1 lb 9 oz/700 g tomatoes, charred under the broiler, peeled, and seeded
handful of corn tortilla chips, crushed
several large handfuls of purslane, cut into bite-size lengths
½ lime
lime wedges, to serve

Purslane is terribly fashionable, due to its unique flavor and healthy dose of omega-3 fatty acids. It is a weed, and beloved by the Mexicans, who stew it as well as eat it raw.

Combine the lime juice, half the garlic, the herbs, cumin, and salt to taste in a nonmetallic bowl. Rub the mixture over the chicken, cover, and let marinate in the refrigerator for at least 1 hour or overnight.

Place the chiles in a pan and pour the boiling water over them. Cover and let stand for 30 minutes until softened. Remove the stalks and seeds. Purée the chiles in a food processor or blender, adding just enough of the stock to make a smooth paste. Stir in the remaining stock.

Heat a tablespoon of the oil in a heavy-bottomed skillet. Add the chile purée with the tomatoes and remaining garlic. Cook over medium heat, stirring, until it has thickened and reduced by about half. Set aside.

Remove the chicken from the marinade, reserving any marinade juices. Heat the remaining oil in a flameproof casserole and brown the chicken. Add any reserved marinade juices and the reduced sauce. Cover and simmer over low heat for 30 minutes, or until the chicken is tender.

Stir the crushed tortilla chips into the sauce and cook for a few minutes. Stir in the purslane, season to taste with salt and pepper, and squeeze over the juice from the lime. Heat through, then serve with lime wedges.

duck with mole sauce & pineapple

serves 4

15 minutes,
plus 2 hours marinating

50 minutes

1 duck, cut into 4 pieces
juice of 2 limes
½ cup pineapple juice
5–8 garlic cloves, sliced or chopped
few shakes of mild red chili powder,
  such as ancho
salt

2 tbsp sugar
2 cups Mole Poblano
  (see page 91)
½ pineapple, peeled and cut into
  slices
fresh chile strips, to garnish

A wonderful combination of sweetness and spiciness, this dish is bursting with Mexican flavors. Serve with a mixture of long-grain and wild rice for a sophisticated touch.

Combine the duck with the lime juice, pineapple juice, garlic, chili powder, salt to taste, and half the sugar in a shallow nonmetallic dish. Cover with plastic wrap and let marinate in the refrigerator for at least 2 hours, or preferably overnight.

Preheat the oven to 325°F/160°C. Remove the duck from the marinade and pat dry with paper towels. Arrange the dark meat pieces in a roasting pan and roast in the preheated oven for 20 minutes. Pour off the fat as it renders from the duck.

Add the breast pieces to the pan and continue to roast slowly for an additional 20 minutes. Pour off the fat. Increase the oven temperature to 400°F/200°C and roast for an additional 5–10 minutes, or until the duck is crisp and brown.

Warm the mole sauce in a pan with enough water to prevent it sticking and burning. Set aside and keep warm.

Preheat the broiler. Sprinkle the pineapple with the remaining sugar. Cook under the hot broiler on both sides until the pineapple is lightly browned.

Serve the duck portions accompanied by the pineapple slices and topped with the mole sauce. Garnish with chile strips and serve.

turkey with mole

serves 4

15 minutes

1 hour 40 minutes

4 turkey portions, each cut into 4 pieces

about 2 cups chicken stock, plus extra for thinning

about 1 cup water

1 onion, chopped

1 whole garlic bulb, divided into cloves and peeled

1 celery stalk, chopped

1 bay leaf

1 bunch fresh cilantro, finely chopped

2¼ cups Mole Poblano (see page 91) or use ready-made mole paste, thinned as instructed on the container

4–5 tbsp sesame seeds, to garnish

In Mexican grocery shops you can buy a jar of mole paste—useful for when you don't have a stash of leftover homemade mole sauce in your refrigerator or freezer.

Preheat the oven to 375°F/190°C. Arrange the turkey in a large flame-proof casserole. Pour the stock and water around the turkey, then add the onion, garlic, celery, bay leaf, and half the cilantro.

Cover and bake in the preheated oven for 1–1½ hours, or until the turkey is very tender. Add extra liquid if needed.

Warm the mole sauce in a pan with enough stock to make it the consistency of thin cream.

To toast the sesame seeds for the garnish, place the seeds in an unoiled skillet and dry-fry, shaking the skillet, until lightly golden.

Arrange the turkey pieces on a serving plate and spoon the warmed mole sauce over the top. Sprinkle with the toasted sesame seeds and the remaining chopped cilantro and serve.

desserts & beverages

Mexico is a land that swelters in the heat of the sun, and living there one
needs constant refreshment and rehydration. The cuisine offers a wealth
of drinks to slake this thirst, to refresh, and to replenish—drinks based
on juices or fruits mixed with milk. For a drink with a bit more punch, try one
of the tequila-based Classic Margaritas (see page 254), and on the soothing
side, relax with a traditional Mexican Hot Chocolate (see page 250).

For dessert, the amazing fragrant and sweet fresh fruits of Mexico are
often all you'll want, especially after the hearty and satisfying fare of this
land. If you yearn for something rich, however, try Churros (see page 244)
—cinnamon-scented, doughnut-like fritters—or little meringues named
after the sighs of the nuns who created them.

aztec oranges

serves 4–6

15 minutes

–

6 oranges
1 lime
2 tbsp tequila
2 tbsp orange-flavored liqueur

brown sugar, to taste
fine lime rind strips, to decorate
(see Cook's Tip)

Simplicity itself, this refreshing orange dessert is hard to beat and is the perfect follow-up to a hearty, spiced main course dish.

cook's tip

To make the decoration, finely pare the rind from a lime using a vegetable peeler, then cut into thin strips. Add to boiling water and blanch for 2 minutes. Drain in a strainer and rinse under cold running water. Drain again and pat dry with paper towels. Use this method for decorative orange and lemon strips as well.

Using a sharp knife, cut a slice off the top and bottom of the oranges, then remove the peel and pith, cutting downward and taking care to retain the shape of the oranges.

Holding the oranges on their side, cut them horizontally into slices.

Place the oranges in a nonmetallic bowl. Cut the lime in half and squeeze over the oranges. Sprinkle with the tequila and liqueur, then sprinkle over sugar to taste.

Cover and chill until ready to serve, then transfer to a serving dish and garnish with lime rind strips.

strawberries & oranges with lime

serves 4

15 minutes

–

3 sweet oranges
1½ cups strawberries
grated rind and juice of 1 lime
1–2 tbsp superfine sugar

to decorate
fine lime rind strips (see page 233)
fresh mint sprig

Ideal as a summery dessert, this dish can also be served as a fresh fruit dish with brunch. The oranges enhance the delicate flavor of the berries.

Using a sharp knife, cut a slice off the top and bottom of the oranges, then remove the peel and pith, cutting downward and taking care to retain the shape of the oranges.

Using a small sharp knife, cut down between the membranes of the oranges to remove the segments. Discard the membranes.

Hull the strawberries, pulling the leaves off with a pinching action. Cut into slices, along the length of the strawberries.

Place the oranges and strawberries in a nonmetallic bowl, then sprinkle with the lime rind and juice and sugar. Cover and chill until ready to serve.

To serve, transfer to a serving bowl. Decorate the dish with lime rind strips and a mint sprig.

cook's tip

An optional hit of orange-flavored liqueur is delicious—reduce or omit the sugar.

variation

Replace the oranges with mangoes, and the strawberries with blackberries, for a dramatically colored dessert.

icy fruit blizzard

serves 4

15 minutes,
plus 2 hours freezing

–

1 pineapple
1 large piece seeded watermelon, peeled and cut into small pieces
1 ½ cups strawberries or other berries, hulled and left whole or sliced

1 mango, peach, or nectarine, peeled and sliced
1 banana, peeled and sliced
orange juice
superfine sugar, to taste

Keep a store of prepared fruits in the freezer, then whizz up into this refreshing dessert, which is as light and healthy as it is satisfying. You can vary the fruits as you like.

Cover 2 nonstick cookie sheets or ordinary cookie sheets with a sheet of plastic wrap. Arrange the fruits on top and open freeze for at least 2 hours, or until firm and icy.

Place one type of fruit in a food processor and process until it is all broken up into small pieces.

Add a little orange juice and sugar to taste, and continue to process until it forms a granular mixture. Repeat with the remaining fruits. Arrange in chilled bowls and serve immediately.

cook's tip

The fruits can be processed all together, if preferred, or use just one type of fruit—match the juice to the fruit.

variation

For an icy fruit yogurt shake, omit the pineapple and watermelon and process the remaining fruits together, replacing the juice with a half-and-half mix of milk and fruit yogurt.

bunuelo stars

 serves 4

 5–10 minutes

 5–10 minutes

4 flour tortillas
3 tbsp ground cinnamon
6–8 tbsp superfine sugar
vegetable oil, for frying

to serve
chocolate ice cream
fine orange rind strips (see page 233)

Cutting the flour tortillas into star shapes makes a whimsical treat, and the points of the stars get deliciously crisp.

Using a sharp knife or kitchen scissors, cut each tortilla into star shapes.

Mix the cinnamon and sugar together in a bowl and set aside.

Heat 1 inch/2.5 cm of oil in a shallow, wide skillet until it is hot enough to brown a cube of bread in 30 seconds. Working one at a time, fry the star shapes until one side is golden, then turn and cook until golden on the other side. Remove from the hot oil with a slotted spoon and drain on paper towels.

Sprinkle generously with the cinnamon and sugar mixture. Serve with chocolate ice cream, sprinkled with orange rind strips.

cook's tip

These star-shaped bunuelos make an attractive decoration for an ice-cream sundae with Mexican flavors—caramel, cinnamon, coffee, and chocolate.

variation

Drench the bunuelos in a simple syrup, flavored with a little cinnamon or anise.

empanadas of banana & chocolate

serves 4–6

10 minutes

15 minutes

about 8 sheets of phyllo pastry, cut in half lengthwise

melted butter or vegetable oil, for brushing

2 ripe sweet bananas

1–2 tsp sugar

juice of ¼ lemon

6–7 oz/175–200 g semisweet chocolate, broken into small pieces

confectioners' sugar, for dusting

ground cinnamon, for dusting

Using phyllo pastry makes these empanadas light and crisp on the outside, while the filling of diced banana and pieces of chocolate melt into a scrumptious hot banana-chocolate goo.

cook's tip

You could use ready-made puff pastry instead of phyllo for a more puffed-up effect.

Preheat the oven to 375°F/190°C. Working one at a time, lay a long rectangular sheet of phyllo out in front of you and brush it with butter.

Peel and dice the bananas and place in a bowl. Add the sugar and lemon juice and stir well to combine. Stir in the chocolate.

Place a couple of teaspoons of the banana and chocolate mixture in one corner of the dough, then fold over into a triangle shape to enclose the filling. Continue to fold in a triangular shape, until the phyllo is completely wrapped around the filling.

Dust the pockets with confectioners' sugar and cinnamon. Place on a cookie sheet and continue the process with the remaining phyllo and filling.

Bake in the oven for 15 minutes, or until the pastries are golden. Remove from the oven and serve hot—warn people that the filling is very hot.

churros

serves 4

10 minutes

15 minutes

1 cup water

rind of 1 lemon

6 tbsp butter

⅛ tsp salt

generous ¾ cup all-purpose flour

¼ tsp ground cinnamon, plus extra
   for dusting

½–1 tsp vanilla extract

3 eggs

vegetable oil, for frying

superfine sugar, for dusting

Sold on the streets of Mexico, these tempting treats can be enjoyed at any time of the day—dip them into a cup of hot chocolate for breakfast, nibble them as a midday snack with coffee, or serve them as part of a late-night supper.

Place the water with the lemon rind in a heavy-bottomed pan. Bring to a boil, add the butter and salt, and cook the mixture for a few moments until the butter melts.

Add the flour all at once with the cinnamon and vanilla extract, then remove the pan from the heat and stir rapidly until it forms the consistency of mashed potatoes.

Beat in the eggs, one at a time, using a wooden spoon; if you have difficulty incorporating the eggs to a smooth mixture, use a potato masher, then when it is mixed, return to a wooden spoon and mix until smooth.

Heat 1 inch/2.5 cm of oil in a deep skillet until it is hot enough to brown a cube of bread in 30 seconds.

Place the batter in a pastry bag fitted with a wide star tip, then squeeze out 5-inch/13-cm lengths directly into the hot oil, making sure that the churros are about 3–4 inches/7.5–10 cm apart, as they will puff up as they cook. You may need to fry them in 2 or 3 batches.

Cook the churros in the hot oil for 2 minutes on each side, until they are golden brown. Remove with a slotted spoon and drain on paper towels.

Dust generously with sugar and sprinkle with cinnamon to taste. Serve either hot or at room temperature.

torta de cielo

serves 4–6

15 minutes,
plus 30 minutes cooling

40–50 minutes

1 cup unsalted butter, at room
   temperature, plus extra for
   greasing

1¼ cups whole almonds, in
   their skins

1¼ cups sugar

3 eggs, lightly beaten

1 tsp almond extract

1 tsp vanilla extract

9 tbsp all-purpose flour

pinch of salt

to decorate

confectioners' sugar, for dusting
slivered almonds, toasted

*This flat almond-flavored sponge
cake has a dense, moist texture
which melts in the mouth. The
perfect accompaniment to a good
strong cup of coffee.*

Preheat the oven to 350°F/180°C. Lightly grease an 8-inch/20-cm round
or square cake pan and line the pan with parchment paper.

Place the almonds in a food processor and process to form a "mealy"
mixture. Set aside.

Beat the butter and sugar together in a large bowl until smooth and fluffy.
Beat in the eggs, almonds, and both the almond and vanilla extracts until
well blended.

Stir in the flour and salt and mix briefly, until the flour is just incorporated.

Pour or spoon the batter into the prepared pan and smooth the surface.
Bake in the preheated oven for 40–50 minutes, or until the cake feels
spongy when gently pressed.

Remove from the oven and let stand on a wire rack to cool. To serve, dust
with confectioners' sugar and decorate with toasted slivered almonds.

mexican chocolate meringues

makes about 25 meringues

10 minutes,
plus 1 hour cooling

2 hours

4–5 egg whites, at room temperature
pinch of salt
1/4 tsp cream of tartar
1/4–1/2 tsp vanilla extract
about 1 cup superfine sugar
1/8–1/4 tsp ground cinnamon
4 oz/115 g semisweet chocolate,
    grated

to serve

ground cinnamon
generous 3/4 cup strawberries
chocolate-flavored cream
    (see Cook's Tip)

The Mexican name for these delicate meringues is suspiros, meaning "sighs"—supposedly the contented sighs of the nuns who created them. They are lightly crisp on the outside, with deliciously chewy centers.

cook's tip

To make the flavored cream, simply stir half-melted chocolate pieces into stiffly whipped cream, then chill until firm.

Preheat the oven to 300°F/150°C. Whisk the egg whites until they are foamy, then add the salt and cream of tartar and beat until very stiff. Whisk in the vanilla extract, then slowly whisk in the sugar, a small amount at a time, until the meringue is shiny and stiff. This should take about 3 minutes by hand, and under a minute with an electric beater.

Whisk in the cinnamon and grated chocolate. Spoon mounds of about 2 tablespoonfuls on to an ungreased nonstick cookie sheet. Space the mounds well.

Bake in the preheated oven for 2 hours, or until set.

Carefully remove from the cookie sheet. If the meringues are too moist and soft, return them to the oven to firm up and dry out more. Let cool completely.

Serve the chocolate meringues dusted with cinnamon and accompanied by strawberries and chocolate-flavored cream.

soothing mexican drinks

serves 4

10 minutes

10 minutes

strawberry milkshake

3 cups strawberries

3 cups milk

1 cup strawberry yogurt (optional)

sugar, to taste

2 handfuls of ice cubes

mexican hot chocolate

4–6 oz/115–175 g semisweet
   chocolate, broken into small pieces

½ tsp ground cinnamon

4 cups milk

dash of almond extract

dash of vanilla extract

just a few grains of salt (to bring out
   the flavor of the chocolate)

superfine sugar, to taste

2 tbsp grated chocolate

4 cinnamon sticks, to serve (optional)

Two milky drinks, packed with authentic Mexican flavors—choose a cooling strawberry milkshake for a hot summer's day, or a rich hot chocolate drink, with spicy aromas, as a winter warmer.

variation

To vary the flavor of the milkshake, substitute raspberries, bananas, or mango for the strawberries and use a yogurt of your choice.

To make the strawberry milkshake, place half the strawberries in a food processor or blender, reserving 4 for decoration. Add half the milk and yogurt, if using, and process to a purée.

Add sugar to taste and half the ice cubes, then process again until the ice is crushed and the drink is thick and icy. Pour into tall glasses, decorate with the reserved strawberries, and serve immediately. Repeat with the remaining ingredients.

To make the mexican hot chocolate, gently heat the chocolate with the cinnamon and milk in a pan.

When the chocolate has melted, add the almond and vanilla extracts with the salt and sugar. Whisk together until the mixture is well blended and heated through.

Pour into cups, sprinkle with grated chocolate, and serve each cup with a cinnamon stick for stirring, if wished.

fruity refreshers

serves 4–6

10 minutes, plus 2 hours
chilling for the sangria

coconut-lime drink

2 cups coconut milk (unsweetened)

1/2 cup freshly squeezed lime juice

4 cups tropical fruit juice, such as
mango, papaya, guava, or passion
fruit

sugar, to taste

crushed ice

fresh mint sprigs, to decorate

sangria

1 bottle dry full-bodied red wine

4 tbsp orange-flavored liqueur

4 tbsp brandy

1 cup orange juice

sugar, to taste

1 orange, washed

1 lime, washed

1 peach or nectarine

1/2 cucumber, thinly sliced

ice cubes

sparkling mineral water, for topping up

*These fragrant, utterly refreshing
drinks are full of the tropical flavors
of Mexico. They cool and revive
with each sip.*

cook's tip

*To turn the Coconut-Lime Drink
into an alcoholic cocktail, add
2 tablespoons of white rum per
person. Add an extra decoration
of tropical fruit pieces, threaded
on to bamboo skewers.*

To make the Coconut-Lime Drink, combine the coconut milk with the
lime juice, tropical fruit juice, and sugar to taste in a large, nonmetallic
bowl. Add the ice and whisk until well mixed. Alternatively, place the
ingredients in a food processor or blender and process until well mixed.
Pour into tall glasses and serve immediately, decorated with mint sprigs.

To make the Sangria, pour the wine into a punch bowl and mix in the
liqueur, brandy, orange juice, and sugar to taste. Cover and let chill in the
refrigerator for at least 2 hours.

Just before serving, slice the orange and lime widthwise. Cut the peach in
half, remove the pit, and slice the flesh.

Remove the punch bowl from the refrigerator. Add the prepared fruits,
cucumber, and ice cubes and top up with mineral water. Serve at once.

classic margaritas

serves 2

10 minutes

–

classic margaritas

pared lime or lemon rind

salt, for dipping

3 tbsp tequila

3 tbsp orange-flavored liqueur

3 tbsp freshly squeezed lime juice

handful of cracked ice

fine lime rind strips (see page 233),
   to decorate

melon margaritas

1 small flavorful cantaloupe melon
   peeled, seeded, and diced

several large handfuls of ice

juice of 1 lime

generous ⅓ cup tequila

sugar, to taste

frozen peach margaritas

1 peach, pitted, sliced, and frozen,
   or an equal amount of ready-
   frozen peaches

4 tbsp tequila

4 tbsp peach or orange-flavored
   liqueur

juice of ½ lime

1–2 tbsp fresh peach or orange juice,
   if needed

*Margaritas are what make a
hot and sultry Mexican afternoon
not only tolerable but something
to look forward to. A tropical
holiday in a glass.*

To make the classic margaritas, moisten the rim of 2 shallow, stemmed glasses with the lime rind, then dip the edge of the glasses in salt. Shake off the excess.

Place the tequila in a food processor or blender with the liqueur, lime juice, and cracked ice. Process to blend well.

Pour the drink into the prepared glasses, taking care not to disturb the salt-coated rim. If preferred, strain the drink before pouring into the glass. Decorate with lime rind strips and serve.

To make the melon margaritas, place the melon in a food processor or blender and process to a purée. Add the ice, lime juice, tequila, and sugar to taste and process until smooth. Pour into chilled shallow glasses.

To make the frozen peach margaritas, blend the frozen fruit, tequila, liqueur, and lime juice in a food processor or blender to a thick purée. If too thick, add a little diced peach or orange juice to thin. Pour into chilled glasses and serve.